How to ... Reproduce Your Church

Helpful hints on church planting
and pitfalls to be avoided

Timothy Starr
and
Gary V Carter

Copyright © 1985, 2009 by Kainos Enterprises

All rights reserved. No part of this book may be reproduced in any form or by any electronic or mechanical means, including information storage and retrieval systems, without permission in writing from the publisher, except by a reviewer who may quote brief passages in a review.

Published By: Kainos Enterprises
7777 Churchville Road
Brampton Ontario Canada L6Y 0H3

ISBN: 978-0-9685427-3-6

Contents

Preface to the 2009 Reprint 5
About the Authors 7
Introduction 9
1 Why Start A New Church? 11
2 What Does the Bible Have to Say? 27
    I. The Great Commission 28
    II. The Biblical Example 31
    III. The Principle of Reproduction 32
    IV. The Principle of Sending 33
    V. The Principle of Giving 35
    VI. The Principle of Faith 36
    VII. The Principle of Imitation 36
3 Problems or Possibilities? 39
    Supposed Problems 39
    Potential Problems 42
    Real Problems 44
    Questions for the Local Congregation 48
    Questions for the Pastor 50
4 Is There a Procedure That Works? 53
    Phase I: Inspiration 54
    Phase II: Investigation 54
    Phase III: Information 55
    Phase IV: Intention 61
    Phase V: Inception 62
5 What About Those Prototypes? 65
    1. Pastor led daughter churches 68
    2. People led daughter churches 71
    3. Association led daughter churches 72
    4. Association led churches with a denominational board ... 72
    5. Daughter churches formed through a "Macedonian Call" ... 74
    6. Cooperating versus opposing daughter churches 76
    7. Daughters started through adoption 77
    8. Daughters born through relocation 78
6 Sounds Good, But What Now? 81
7 Twenty Questions Answered 93
A Lesson in Church Anatomy 103

Preface to the 2009 Reprint

A lot has changed since 1986 when this book was first published.

Billy Graham was in his prime. Rick Warren was unknown.

Few understood the difference between software and hardware. The fax machine was unknown.

Homosexual marriage was unthinkable. Stem cell research not even a dream.

That was then. This is now.

Obviously much has changed in 20 years. And it continues to change. Joel Osteen is the new rising star and Rick Warren is the veteran. Billy Graham has faced his last campaign. It is no longer just Internet but it is wireless Internet and even radio is moving to satellite radio.

As I reviewed this document I decided not to change anything. You will have to interpret in the light of new circumstances as they unfold. You will notice that the experience cited is all Canadian and the descriptions and figures are naturally all out of date. Actually, I don't know all the people referenced in this book because Timothy played a major part in the writing. And some old timers will recognize names of the past. The Lord knows who these people are and we give honor to their service in His name.

Timothy Starr is now over 80 years old. Over 150 churches were planted on his watch. I became the beneficiary of the collective wisdom developed in that pursuit. For years, I have been taking a different tack. We have helped hundreds, perhaps thousands of churches.

Now I am back at focusing on tools specifically designed for starting churches. This is more difficult.

Let me explain. It is not difficult conceptually. But it is difficult to build tools for church starting because of the limited interest. By way of illustration, Internet searches for the term "church" in one day number 1,977. Searches for "Joel Osteen" number 1,732. Searches for "church planting" numbered 67. And it changes by the minute. Rick Warren is down to 344. Apparently, Rick is getting to be old news. Apart from the volatility in the marketplace, Church Planting is a very small marketplace. In fact, on most days, searches for "pet rock" out number the searches for "church planting" by a 2 to 1 margin. And every month, "lawn sprinkler" out searches "Great Commission." Internet searches do give a snapshot of what people around the globe are interested in.

So what is so hard? As yet we have no subsidies from deep pockets. Development of churches is very expensive and the resources for the cause are very expensive as well. We could do it much faster if there was money available to pay a living wage to the developers.

Please pray that the Lord will move a heart or two to supply the millions of dollars necessary to build the tools church starting leaders need for today and tomorrow!

Gary V Carter

About the Authors

Gary Carter was born and raised in Toronto. He and his wife, Wendy, have two daughters and two sons. Pastor Carter is a graduate of Ontario Bible College with the B.R.E. and B.Th. degrees. He has been in the pastorate thirteen years, as well as serving as Field Representative for the David C. Cook Publishing Company for two years. The material in this book stems from his personal involvement as the founding pastor of the Eastwood Baptist Church, an extension work of Faith Baptist Church, St. Thomas, Ontario.

Timothy Starr's ministry of direction, counsel and encouragement has led to the planting of over one hundred Canadian churches. Since 1971 he has served with The Fellowship of Evangelical Baptist Churches in Canada, first as Field Representative and now as Secretary of the Home Mission Board. He and his wife, Hazel, have raised a family of two sons and two daughters. Dr. Starr is a graduate of Toronto Bible College and has a Doctor of Ministry from Luther Rice Seminary.

Introduction

It's always church planting time in North America. Springtime, summer, fall or winter — seeds of new churches are being sown across our vast continent.

Planting methods may vary. Many churches begin with a prayer group which then expands into a full-blown ministry in a community. Others start as the result of the vision of one individual who sees the need of his particular area.

One of the finest methods of church planting is the parent/daughter concept, whereby a church commissions a number of its families to launch a daughter work in a nearby community.

We know that for all our planting and our watering, it is God who gives the increase, but He expects us to take these initial steps of sowing the seed and cultivating the young plant. No matter what the season, this work must go on to assure continuing growth in churches and in souls won to Christ.

This book has been written for the express purpose of motivating, encouraging and educating local churches in reproduction. It is the conviction of the authors that every organized church, sooner or later, should sponsor a new church. May God use these pages to challenge your church into a reproductive ministry.

1

Why Start A New Church?

What's that? You can't expect a local church to encourage a group of its families to leave and form a new church! Well, that is what this book is all about. Church reproduction happens when a church catches a vision of a needy area and seeks to do something about it. One way of accomplishing this is to encourage a number of families to consider starting a local church in that particular area.

If this unexpected event is ever to take place, certain definite, concrete factors must be started in order to encourage the launching of a daughter or extension church. Our churches must see the need and the advantages of reproduction.

Naturally the first reason should be the most significant: it is a command of our Lord. In the great commission (Matthew 28:18-20), believers are instructed to disciple new converts. This includes bringing people into the fellowship of a local church. Now, do we stop with our own local church? Are we content to carry out this command solely through missionary support to other countries? Or do we seek out border communities to ours and nearby towns in which to open up local churches?

One can readily see that the great commission embraces non-churched communities. It extends to communities lacking sufficient evangelical witness. But how will these areas be reached if no local church is present to evangelize? It is reasonable to suggest that this is the responsibility of the nearest church. Even more important, it is imperative that a local church seek to carry out the mandate of Jesus Christ, both at home and abroad.

This brings us to a second consideration, that church planting fosters evangelism. It is essential for every beginning church to see new people being brought into its membership through faith in Jesus Christ. We all know of Christian families who drive miles to attend a particular church, often passing several others on their way. They, themselves, are being ministered to, but what about their neighbours? Is it not true that the average nominal Christian, as well as the non Christian, can better be reached by a church that is nearby? And does it not follow logically that those four or five families who drive out of their community each week to worship would be more effective in forming a Bible study and prayerfully considering opening a work in their own neighbourhood?

In the early 1970s, several families from Dovercourt Baptist Church in Toronto moved to Alliston, Ontario. Although they drove the thirty or so miles to Dovercourt for a period of time, it soon became evident that it was too far to get their non Christian neighbours to come with them. This led these families to cooperate with others to form what is today the Grace Baptist Church, a congregation of two hundred, reaching out to the people of Alliston.

It should not be assumed that because there is a church in any given community, that community is going to be reached for Christ. All too many assemblies are out of touch with the people and the needs of their community, with the result that many are simply brick structures passed daily by those who have no understanding of their purpose. Yet it can be stated with some assurance that if an active church is located within a community, the people of that church will have a better opportunity to develop meaningful relationships with the residents than those who would come from the outside. They will learn the needs of the people as they live with them, and will develop their programs and ministries accordingly.

Keith M. Bailey, one of the executives of the Christian and Missionary Alliance Churches, studied the growth pattern of his denomination and concluded, "Statistics show that the new congregations are seeing a proportionately greater harvest of souls than the established churches. Every new church planted extends the cutting edge of evangelism."[1]

Church reproduction is a growth strategy. Multitudes of churches have experienced starting a daughter church, even commissioning some of their finest families to participate in the branch work, only to find that within a few weeks their facilities were filled again. Within a year of the formation of a new work, the total attendance of the two churches generally far exceeds the attendance of the parent church before the extension work got underway.

In 1972, Temple Baptist Church, Sarnia, Ontario, was running from four to five hundred in the morning services. In that year approximately fifty members left to open Huron Park Baptist Church. Within a matter of weeks, Temple Baptist was again packed to capacity.

In 1979, Bluewater Baptist Church got underway as a second daughter work from Temple, with about sixty people being commissioned. Again, within a matter of weeks Temple Baptist was packed out. In 1985 erected a new auditorium to seat 1000. Total attendance in all three churches today runs over eight hundred in the morning services.

Cloverdale Baptist Church, Surrey, B.C., is fifty years old. During its ministry, this church has fostered five daughter churches. In the fall of 1981 it opened a million dollar structure with seating capacity of approximately nine hundred. Starting daughter churches has not deterred the growth of Cloverdale.

There have been times, of course, when a parent/daughter ministry has not worked out to a net gain within a year, but it would appear that this is the exception rather than the rule.

Church reproduction is a healthy stimulant to the mother church, too. Of necessity, positions such as deacon, treasurer, Sunday school superintendent, etc. need to be filled. So when key leaders leave to launch an extension work, other members are called upon to fill the vacuum. Perhaps the new officers may not do the jobs as well at the start, but with time, training and proper reinforcement, they might well grow into their positions and serve with distinction. By church reproduction, many who were not totally involved are motivated to share their gifts and talents.

In one community a church was involved in a problem that eventually led to serious division. The core leadership, including the majority of deacons, over half the Sunday school staff and other workers, left to form a new church. Within a month or two new leadership stepped forward in the first church, and soon every vacant position was occupied. Today there are two aggressive churches in that community. Whereas before the one church had two hundred in the morning services, today the original work has grown to two hundred and fifty, while the new church averages well over the hundred mark.

Mission work is fostered, both in personnel and in church reproduction. Studies by various denominational church extension departments, reveal that the new churches, over the course of time will return far more in mission and denominational support than they have received in grant support.

In January, 1985, Forest Hills Baptist Church, Dartmouth, N. S., drew up their new budget. It indicated that various mission agencies of The Fellowship of Evangelical Baptist Churches in Canada would receive a total of $15,000. This was a Home Mission church in the early 1970s. There was not a year when that church received $15,000 in grant support. Yet now, one decade later, it is giving this amount to the parent body. Statistics indicate that this is typical.

New churches, with their exciting growth and development, have a way of producing candidates for both pastoral and missionary work. Temple Baptist Church, Lower Sackville, N.S. started in 1976 with only the pastor and his wife, Don and Janice Robins. Today there is a thriving congregation of close to three hundred. Already that church has produced three pastors with two more in training. There appears to be something about a new challenge that brings with it an incentive to apply for the ministry, both at home and abroad.

The very insufficiency of churches in our communities makes church reproduction a necessity. Looking over the new developing subdivisions of our major cities, one must ask, where are the churches to meet the spiritual needs of the residents? In Vaughan City, bordering the northern part of Toronto, fifty thousand residents have moved into new homes since 1980. In 1985 there was not a single church building of any denomination. This is one of at least twelve developing communities in Canadian cities where there is a dire need for churches to be planted. One can only speculate on the limitless opportunities in the United States.

Mission boards also must not overlook the growing multicultural population evident in our North American cities. The Toronto Star published the following chart on August 21, 1985, showing that only sixty-eight percent of Toronto residents claimed English as their mother tongue. The figures were released by the Ontario Ministry of Citizenship and Culture, based on the 1981 census.

Metro Toronto's multilingual society

Mother Tongue	Population	Percent of Total	%1971-85 Change
English	1,447,155	67.71	- 1.84
French	32,115	1.50	- 13.87
Italian	176,450	8.26	- 15.07
Portuguese	63,225	2.96	+ 82.68
German	40,190	1.88	- 23.45
Chinese	60,275	2.82	+190.27
Greek	46,125	2.16	+ 7.52
Ukrainian	29,340	1.37	- 6.66
Yugoslav*	21,415	1.00	- 6.34
Polish	28,000	1.31	- 3.50
Indo-Pakistani**	26,415	1.24	+290.47
Spanish	21,665	1.01	+227.02
Hungarian	17,615	0.82	- 5.50
All Other	127,410	5.96	+ 22.83
Total	2,137,395	100.00	+ 2.31

* Yugoslav includes: Yugoslav, Croatian, Serbian, Slovenian and Yugoslav N.O.S.

** Indo-Pakistani Includes: Bengali, Cingalese, Hindi, Malayalam, Tamil, Telugu, Urdu, Indo-Pakistani N.O.S.

Now if this is true of Toronto, what about Montreal, Vancouver and the major American cities? Yes, our churches have a mission field at home, in fact, for many churches, right at the front door!

The church is eager to send a missionary to the Philippines or Japan. Why not to an ethnic group within their own city? There will not be the same romance of a tearful farewell at the airport, but the need is just as great.

It is hard to understand how one church, located in the heart of an Italian district, would give thousands of dollars to overseas missions, but have no outreach to the ethnic population of their own community. To my knowledge, no attempt has ever been made to secure an Italian worker. Before long this church will be forced to close because of losses being suffered annually;

but there has been no effort made toward a transition that would provide ministry for the people of the area.

Attention must be given to the high density apartment complexes located in large urban centres. St. James Town, located in the heart of Toronto, is made up of eight separate apartments with about 25,000 people. Surely some denominational board or local church could sponsor a new work by means of renting an apartment or developing a number of cell groups.

It was Dr. Robert Lee who saw the need of urban communities and wrote, "If we do not become as evangelicals involved in the city, we will be standing on the sidewalk watching the parade march by."

Smaller towns and communities must not be overlooked either. Several years ago a group of pastors of the Quinte Association (eastern Ontario) met to discuss the spiritual needs of the geographic area for which they were responsible. Within a matter of two hours they had come up with six areas in which a Bible study should be started as the forerunner of a future church. That very day churches were assigned specific areas closest to their field. There must be thousands of communities in North America where a new church is needed.

And what about the collegiate population? Here the leaders of tomorrow's society are being trained today. Evangelicals have little presence on or near our major Canadian educational centres. It is recognized that students cannot maintain a church. Their finances are limited; their school year is only nine months in duration. Nevertheless, this is a mission field. There is an opportunity for teachers and interested families to open a church with this specialized ministry in mind.

There are developing ministries, too, in the residences of senior citizens housing. Almost ten percent of the present population of North America is comprised of people sixty-five years and older. By the turn of the century the figure is estimated to be twelve percent. More and more, institutions will be designed and programs structured to meet the needs of these older people. The presence of the church is indeed important in this area of service.

There are striking examples of these residences across Canada today. The Baptist Foundation of British Columbia has erected seven such institutions. Westbourne Baptist Church, Calgary, for a number of years has been housing a large number of seniors. The Fellowship Towers in Toronto has a resident population of over three hundred. Located in the heart of the business and commercial district, the Towers offers a full range of services to its residents, and has, in addition, a church within its premises. There will be an even greater need of such residences in the 1990s.

It can be said without contradiction that the opportunities for planting new churches are indeed limitless. North America needs more churches to handle the diverse needs of its people from the varied cultures, races and lifestyles that exist.

Church reproduction becomes vital when one considers the number of churches that close each year, often with the result that all gospel witness is removed from the community. The Fellowship of Evangelical Baptist Churches in Canada has an affiliation of close to five hundred churches. Each year one to three of these churches will cease to exist. That means that the same number of new churches must be started each year just to maintain the status quo. This has been taking place among the British Baptist Churches in England, and because they have not been heavily involved in church planting, there are now few Baptist churches in the British Isles than at the turn of the century.

Yet while this aggressive program of new church planting is going on, there needs to be greater attention given to helping such churches in crisis. Mind you, many urban churches in crisis have a terminal illness, but either do not know it or are unwilling to admit it! Whole sectors or metropolitan areas have changed rapidly. The movement of people, the physical deterioration of whole districts, the breakdown of a sense of community and the social and economic changes have produced real trauma for churches in these areas.

The outward migration of people from the inner city has resulted in the depletion of wise and good leadership. It has also reduced financial support. Yet human needs have increased, making it more difficult for the pastor and the remaining members to continue the ministry as before. Yet with all that, there is the desire for "business as usual." Older members refer wistfully to the "good old days."

Another problem that arises in these churches is that when numbers are reduced, so is the pastoral staff. Yet their missionary support continues, many times without reduction. It would appear that mission becomes foremost, even ahead of the survival of the church. Yet if these churches close, what will happen to the mission dollar? Churches in crisis have to develop a whole new line of thinking in defining "missions."

Bold Mission Thrust of the Southern Baptist Convention defined a church as being in crisis when its current programs of outreach and ministry are no longer effective in reaching and nurturing people for Christ, and it has not learned to adapt the traditional programs or develop new programs. We need to understand some of the reasons that bring a church into a crisis situation.

A significant population shift can lead a church into crisis. During World War II the United States Government built a huge air base at Stevensville, Nfld. Thousands of servicemen with their families moved to the area. An American Baptist group erected a church building and formed a congregation, with the intention of ministering to both the service personnel and those of the local community. But the church never reached the native Newfoundlander, with the result that when the base was closed and the servicemen and their families left, the church closed too. There were no people to attend the services!

Socioeconomic class changes can lead a church into crisis. Toronto's third oldest Baptist church, Dovercourt, met for years in a massive brick structure. For years it had been the site for great rallies and special conventions. When it was built, the area was one of the fashionable sections of the city. That area today is made up of crowded rooming houses filled largely with single parents. In addition there is a large group of mixed ethnic people. Many residents are on welfare. Mothers with young children use daycare centres in order to work. Sensing this change, Dovercourt sold its outdated building and relocated at a new facility designed to meet community needs.

Today the church carries on a varied ministry. Traditional services on Sunday are maintained, along with midweek prayer meeting. In addition, the church has been able to call a full-time youth pastor. A residence for senior citizens provides housing and care for over two hundred. New accommodations have made it possible to branch out into multicultural ministry. A full-time program for the residence provides opportunities for church members to participate.

Actually, this church, like many others, could carry on an even more extensive outreach ministry with a daycare centre for working mothers, a clothing depot for needy people, and a counselling service. But it is continuing to function as a church and is meeting some of the needs of its community.

Racial and ethnic cultural changes can lead a church into crisis. This is where we need to raise up workers from various multicultural backgrounds to minister to their own people, knowing their language, customs and distinctives.

Housing pattern changes, too, can lead a church into crisis. A Christian dentist opened a beautiful church edifice, Eglinton Baptist, in Toronto in the 1940s. It was a show place for its beauty and three story educational plant. Today the community has changed from private residences to huge apartment buildings. A whole new challenge faces that church. It was pathetic to visit the church several years ago and see a small group of people meeting Sunday morning in a back room. The great auditorium, the massive Sunday school building and the parking lot were vacant. Recent pastors have introduced a new type of ministry and the attendance has increased. Once again the facilities are being used.

Land use changes can also lead a church into crisis. In October, 1976, Langstaff Baptist Church, Langstaff, ON, closed when a new highway cut off its community.

I am not suggesting that a local church should never close. There are times when in the plan of God, a local church should cease to exist. If a group of members is not willing to adjust its ministry to the needs of a changing community, perhaps it should close. There are times when members are so contentious, it is right to disband and go their separate ways. There have been times when the community in which a church was located changed from residential to commercial. The church was no longer needed. In other cases, a change of language was needed and a period of closed doors was necessary to bring this about.

Far too many mission dollars have been used to prop up dead programs. Limited home mission funds need to have priority in the spiritual needs of people. Is our business to maintain an institution or an "ecclesia"? Much more effort must be put into developing a congregation sensitive to the real community in which it is attempting to minister.

Each year several local churches merge with other churches. It may appear that merging two struggling churches will make for one strong congregation, or that it is logical for one struggling church to merge into a strong growing church. Strangely enough, however, many churches that merge find that within a short period of time the total attendance has levelled off at the number of the largest of the two churches, resulting in a net decrease. Generally speaking, mergers are not good for numerical church growth.

Merging congregations fail to take into consideration their roots, the bond of fellowship through the years, individuals holding offices and the personal attachment members have to a church building. Much better for a congregation to carefully examine their ministries and to adjust their work to community needs, or to close up and let their assets be used by mission boards willing to carry on an effective outreach.

Floyd Avenue Baptist Church in Toronto had a fine ministry for many years. Then in the late 1960s the community changed from largely English speaking to ethnic. Core leadership of the church was dispersed through job relocation or moves to the suburbs. In 1984 the congregation was reduced to about twenty members, most of them older and not able to carry on effective ministry. The building became a burden to maintain. The people decided to turn over their deed to the Fellowship of Evangelical Baptist Churches, which in turn established a Floyd Avenue Baptist Church Foundation. Today funds from this source are being used to help Fellowship mission boards. And the building, sold to a vibrant growing Chinese church, continues to be the home of ministry to the community. This was a church closure that resulted in a far greater outreach than it could have ever realized had it struggled on with its limited and aging membership. But with all these positive and negative factors, the fact remains that churches do close and churches do merge. So aggressive church reproduction continues to be of utmost importance to growth and development.

Church extension is a necessity, too, because of the small attendances in evangelical churches. Actually, there are not that many people in our churches when you add up the total attendance. The Evangelical Free Church in 1980 had a total of six hundred and fifty churches. Seventy-two percent had fewer than ninety-nine members. The average attendance of Fellowship Baptist churches in Canada is one hundred and twelve. It's easy to see that evangelical churches are really reaching a limited number of people. So if a major part of the population is going to be reached, many more churches will need to be planted, and the present churches will need to expand and enlarge their numerical strength.

Have you noticed how many established churches have a ministry that focuses inward? Their emphasis is almost exclusively for their own members. Many times there is little concern for reaching out to non Christians. This can only be changed when a church takes to heart the great commission of Jesus Christ. A church needs to train and equip its members for a ministry to the world. The ministry to believers is a means to an end, not an end in itself.

Church reproduction can foster this by raising up leaders and sending them out to occupy new communities.

God has entrusted the church today with immense resources, both of talented people and of financial wealth. In evangelical circles there is a large surplus of trained pastors. The Fellowship Baptists well illustrate this. Each year some sixty to eighty men graduate from our schools, expecting to enter the pastorate. With the existing five hundred churches, there is no way, at the present rate of growth, that a quarter of these men will be settled in a Fellowship pulpit in the first year. If, however, in any given year ten percent of the churches would be involved in church reproduction, many of these graduates would soon find a place of service. Mind you, if a man is called to the ministry, he can always open a door by starting a church in some community where there is a spiritual vacuum.

Besides having a surplus of pastors, there is an overflow of finances. Never has the evangelical movement in North America been so affluent. Back in the 1930s, many evangelical churches had a store front building or held their services upstairs over a store. Often a church met in a lodge building where the aroma of booze still lingered from the previous night's activities. Today all that has changed. In many of our cities some of the finest church buildings have been erected by evangelicals. In Canada, it is amazing to see some of the new buildings housing churches of the Pentecostal Assemblies and the Christian and Missionary Alliance denominations.

Today there are finances available for a multitude of ministries such as television, residences for senior citizens, educational institutions and many other enterprises being funded by local churches. It is not uncommon for a congregation of two hundred to have a budget of from $300,000 to $400,000.

Though growing families still have the problem of having sufficient funds to raise a family, there are multitudes of people in their late sixties and above who are wondering what to do with their money. Their children are often well situated, with highly paid positions, and do not need the entire estate of their parents. Churches need to develop a well-defined stewardship program including booklets and films that will encourage Christians to include the work of the local church as part of their last will and testament.

Church reproduction should be taken seriously when you consider that the vast majority of churches reach a point of stagnation by the time they are ten years old. A study taken by The Fellowship of Evangelical Baptist Churches in Canada revealed that seventy-five percent of its churches had reached a point of saturation and were now experiencing less net gain in membership. True, some churches showed a year to year fluctuation, but the church size remained about the same.

We challenge you to study the growth statistics of your church for the past ten years, paying particular attention to conversion growth. Contrast this with biological and transfer growth. Most likely you will be unpleasantly surprised and somewhat disappointed.

Consider the vast numbers of unreached people and you will see the need for church reproduction. On any given Sunday, apart from Christmas and Easter, less than thirty percent of Canadians would be in a service of worship in any denomination. The eastern provinces have a higher percentage of church goers than the western provinces, but even in New Brunswick, the Bible belt of Canada, there is a great potential of unchurched people. It is true that most people will claim some religious preference, but this means little and certainly does not indicate active church attendance.

Finally, church reproduction is a necessity to handle the anticipated increase in population. Our major urban centres will continue to expand and develop. Certain sections of North America are expected to outgrow others. Florida and California are projected to continue to see rapid growth. Vancouver, with its ideal weather, and Toronto, with its industrial base, will continue to lead the growth in Canada. However, most urban centres will see an influx of residents. One church growth specialist has suggested that America will need fifty thousand new churches between now and the turn of the century.

Yes, church growth is essential. Reproduction is a necessity if we are to achieve our goals. But how best can one accomplish this growth?

There are three main ways to start churches today. The pioneer method, as the name implies, starts with an individual who has a burden to open a church. He goes out on his own with little assistance from other churches or people. The Bible Baptist movement in the United States has specialized in training men for this type of church planting, and has been most successful. Dr. Elmer Towns, who works with Dr. Jerry Falwell in Lynchburg, Virginia, has produced a volume entitled, Getting a Church Started. It is really a manual giving the theological foundation and practical techniques of pioneer church planting.

The partnership method is used when a group of churches within an association pull their forces together and start a new work. This, too, is a fine method, although at times the mixture is not always compatible.

But the third method, the parent-daughter concept, is by far the best way to get a church underway. It gives the new church a definite sponsoring body upon which it can depend for support. The mother church is more apt to be involved due to the personal attachment to former members. There is a mutual tie that binds these two together and provides strength to build and to grow.

The other day I heard a pastor of a growing church in Scarborough, Ontario, announce that his church should parent two daughter churches in the next ten years. God bless him—and his people! May their tribe increase!

[1] Bailey, Keith, The Church Planter's Manual, Christian Publications, Inc.

2

What Does the Bible Have to Say?

The concept of daughter churches is biblical. It is not that today's methodology has an exact parallel in the New Testament We would be hard pressed to defend virtually all of our methods on that basis. But the concept of the daughter church fleshes out many of the principles of Scripture in a way that is viable for our generation.

The world in which we live is very different from the first century Roman world. Buildings erected by a variety of "Christian" churches are on many street corners. This is supposed to be a "Christian" land, and what confusion that causes us as we seek to establish and maintain true and exemplary churches!

The distinctions were so much clearer in the embryonic stages of the church. When a local church was started then, no one thought of it in terms of bricks and mortar; they knew that a church was a group of reborn believers, cohesive in a way that was intensely practical, not just intellectual. That very vulnerable sense of interdependence and reliance upon God was shown over and over at the inception of new local churches.

In our western world, new churches are started rather infrequently. Yet the need has never been greater for true, good churches to counterbalance the host of false and poor churches occupying a place of visual dominance in our communities. We need more real churches with potential to reach people where they are emotionally, socially and geographically, and to minister to them in their network of relationships.

We must recapture the vision and vigor of the early believers to plant churches. Let us look at some of the biblical principles behind the successful church planting endeavours of the New Testament and seek to discover how their application relates to the daughter church concept today.

I. The Great Commission

The great commission was the last important word that the Lord Jesus left with His followers before returning to heaven. You will recall that according to Matthew 28:16-20, the command was given to an unproven group of only eleven disciples, yet it had global application. Obviously there was a need to use their resources as efficiently as possible to even begin to get the job done. And despite their limited means, in dependency on the Holy Spirit, we know they did a marvelously effective job for a few generations.

In order to understand our contemporary relationship to these historical facts, let us establish some assumptions of principles we hold in common with the early disciples as we set out to fulfill the great commission.

The first assumption is universality. We must take seriously the responsibility to take the gospel to every creature on planet earth. This presupposes that we cannot rest until all the people in our communities have at least heard the gospel presented effectively enough to know what they are rejecting!

The second assumption is urgency. We must get the job done in the most efficient and expeditious manner, not necessarily the most comfortable!

To state it another way, we must find out what works and pay the price to make it work under God.

The third assumption is the local church is our means. Part of our strategy includes the planting of churches to reach people in new communities, to train them, and to supply a support system for them. We know that the New Testament teaches and implies the essentiality and primacy of the local church. It is obvious, then, that in a place where there is no church, there needs to be one. The only question is how can that church best be established?

If we bind these three assumptions together, it will lead us to an aggressive plan of action, controlled and motivated by the Spirit of God as the agent of our Lord who has already declared His will on the matter. We need never pray, "If it be Thy will," about the great commission! We simply need to get busy and act in faith with the best ideas we can muster which will result in a greater number of prosperous local churches.

All of this, however, ought to be "motherhood and apple pie" to most mature believers. We must look at our own situation not from a theoretical perspective, but with a view to reaching decisions about how to get the job done. We are forced to acknowledge the meager gains we are making in our own generation on this continent. And even though we agree that the "gospel is urgently needed by everyone in our world, we are so protective that we tend to see the fulfillment of the great commission in our community as the exclusive domain of our own local church as it is now constituted. We know of so much more that could occur and should occur in the lives of our own people that a form of myopia blurs our vision to the possibilities beyond our present situation. Maybe we need to take a hard look at what our experience and culture has taught us about the effective church.

Particularly is this true in regard to the subject at hand — the establishing of daughter churches. We find it easy to plead that we are not strong enough or large enough to start another church. Strong enough or large enough compared to what? The church across town? The media mega-church? Or the first century house church without even a complete copy of the Scriptures or believers with any more than a few years' experience in the Lord? Could it be that our churches are stronger and larger than we think? Could it be that the challenge of establishing a new local church in a neighbouring community, or even in our own, might be just the thing needed to express our assumptions in an effective, contemporary strategy?

It appears that too often we have left the planting of new churches to a kind of spontaneous generation. If a family or two gets a vision for a new church we may back their idea — if they are persistent enough. (It is rather more likely that we will resent them as a challenge to the status quo, or as power hungry.) But the great commission also assumes a directed kind of activity which deliberately works at establishing new churches. Initiative must be encouraged in this regard, not resented. In fact, it is to the shame of the leaders in our churches that they don't come up with the idea of a new church first, before someone from the rank and file thinks of it.

The model of sending a missionary or two into an area to establish a church works. By God's grace, men and women have laboured at church planting around the world and God has blessed with new churches. But so often it takes so long to really get the ball rolling, as it were. Why? Could it be that the example and environment provided by a good local church is what is needed to plant a vibrant new church? "By this shall all men know that you are my disciples, if you have love one to another." But if there is no existing group demonstrating this love, how will they get the picture? In other words, the situation seems circular. It is hard to plant a church without having a church to begin with. This problem is particularly acute in our culture, where it is expected that a church will have an age graded program for every family member, a building of its own, a full-time pastor, and all the other "essentials."

If these start-up problems could be eliminated for new churches, then we would have one means of acceleration towards our goal. Establishing daughter churches works to this end. All those who become a part of the new church know that its survival depends upon them as individuals. More personal involvement in effective evangelism is the norm. Concern for the edification of believers is more sharply focused. There is nothing quite like a visible church, located and working in a given community, to fulfill this greatest of commissions. Communities will not be reached unless we "Go." Christ's last command should be our first concern.

II. The Biblical Example

The Apostle Paul was committed to church planting. Wherever he went, local churches sprang up. He sought to reach the major centres with the message of Christ so that the Word of God could fan out to the regions beyond. Thessalonica was a good example. Paul relates in I Thessalonians 1:8 that the message rang out not only in Macedonia and Achaia, but everywhere.

A. Through Home Churches

There are many references in Scripture to groups of believers meeting in homes. The believers in Colossae met in the home of its pastor, Archippus (Philemon 2).

The people of Laodicea met in the home of Nymphas (Colossians 4:15). When Priscilla and Aquila lived in Corinth, they had a gathering of the saints in their home (I Corinthians 16:9). When they were in Ephesus during Paul's extended stay in that city, the church met in their home. Yet a few months later when Paul wrote the epistle to the Romans, near the end of his third missionary journey, we find that Priscilla and Aquila were in Rome. Why? Could it be that he was sending them on ahead to lay the groundwork for his arrival? It seems that this couple was helpful in the establishment of new churches.

Although most homes were small, they were ideal places for new believers to meet together. They could become outposts for evangelism in reaching the communities for Christ.

B. Through Extension

When Paul remained in an area for a prolonged time, he sought to reach into the surrounding areas. While he was at Ephesus on his third missionary journey, it is stated in Acts 19:10 that, "all they who dwelt in Asia heard the word of the Lord Jesus, both Jews and Greeks." Ephesus became a base of operations, and at this time Epaphras was sent back to his home town of Colossae to establish churches in the Lycus valley. It seems that he ministered effectively in a cluster of cities — Colossae, Laodicea and Hierapolis (Colossians 4:13). These cities in Phrygia were evangelized as an extension from Ephesus. Paul's strategy was to have a witness for Christ in every community. This is a good blueprint for us today.

It is significant to notice in these examples of church planting that the reaching out into new areas involved the sending of faithful people from the confines of one local church ministry to another. We have no way of knowing how large a local body of believers was during this period of history. Indications are, however, that since the churches typically met in homes, these churches were obviously not so large that they couldn't physically fit into a house. Perhaps another indicator is that in his writing Paul does not mention a great number of families in connection with any given local church. For example, notice how few Paul baptized in Corinth. There are only three family names mentioned (I Corinthians 1:14-16). And yet, in this context of so few members, there was a willingness, yes even an eagerness to see a church planted in the neighbouring communities. Probably, for Paul, the starting of a "daughter church" involved the sending out of a very few people compared to those we may be able to send today. However, we need to realize that this kind of commissioning involved a significant part of the membership of the mother church. And those people sent must have been some of their very best.

III. The Principle of Reproduction

God made organisms to reproduce. In the Garden of Eden, God said that everything was to reproduce after its kind. As in the physical, so in the spiritual realm. John 15 shows that fruitbearing is a spiritual principle of life. Reproduction is a sign of vigorous health. Normal parents want their children to grow up and be independent. Churches need to reproduce, too. There is a special challenge and blessing which fosters maturity when a church experiences the principle of reproduction. Often daughter churches have the potential to outgrow the size of the mother church. This becomes exciting to both parent and child as our churches expand and we see the fulfillment in reaching our world for Christ.

The principle of reproduction applies on an individual basis as well. We see in the example of Christ and the Apostle Paul the intense desire to impart to their disciples a way of life that exemplified all their qualities of servant leadership and concern for others. Paul's church planting zeal was no doubt included in the "things that thou hast heard of me" which Timothy was to reproduce in "faithful men" whose prime quality would be their ability to "teach others also" (II Timothy 2:2).

On a very practical and contemporary level, there is nothing like the taking on of a big challenge in ministry to motivate our people of greatest potential and stir up their gifts. What more noble task can there be than that of starting a new church? In a new church there are always responsibilities open to people who have never before had the opportunity to stretch in a given area because in the old church someone had (sometimes protectively) filled that place on their behalf. Necessity begets all manner of creative ministry. Often people who have felt less than essential in one body of believers find for themselves a whole new perspective of usefulness in a daughter church.

Pastors and overworked church leaders are often perplexed as to how to get people out of the bleachers and into the game. Starting a new team is an effective way to accomplish this — a new team where front line leadership is needed. It seems that such a thrust would be totally consistent with the reproductory tone of all New Testament ministry.

IV. The Principle of Sending

In our desire to fulfill the great commission, there must always be a blending of the willingness of individuals to initiate service for the Lord in new places with the deliberate sending and commissioning of people to a work.

We acknowledge this to some degree in terms of vocational missionary service, but in most cases we rely on individuals to come up with a vision for service themselves. When the missionary journey of Paul and Barnabas was initiated, according to Acts 13:1-3, however, there appears to have been a group decision of the prophets and teachers in the church at Antioch, clearly instigated by the Holy Spirit, Himself. Even in crass democratic terms, if the idea had come to Paul and Barnabas, they would have had to convince at least one other leader to get a majority vote. The church sent them out. Two of their five leaders is a significant sacrifice. The church deliberately commissioned them to do a job.

We have available to us today a great missionary force of dedicated leaders in our local churches who have wondered about serving God in missions. Sometimes the inhibiting factors of life around them bury this desire. All they have been challenged to think of is vocational missions. They shudder at the thought of leaving established careers to go off to Bible school. And if that doesn't finish them, the spectre of visiting churches for a year or two to raise support from already overstretched missions budgets blows them away. Even the time commitment of a so-called "tentmaking" ministry where they are expected to take pastoral leadership does not seem to fit their potential. If as churches we could see this potential and encourage a few new people to band together as the founding core for a new church, others would join with them and enter into a wonderful adventure of missionary service in one of the truly needy places of this world — our local communities! Here is an available missionary force already sufficiently trained, fully funded by their present vocations, integrated into the networks of the target community, committed and ready to go if (and only if) our churches would catch the vision, take the initiative and turn them loose!

But just as these people are nervous about the difficulties of entering vocational missionary service, so, too, they fear being perceived as divisive or reactionary. Their commitment to the unity of the body, and the stories of past church splits that never seem to die, make them bury their latent desire while they wait for someone else to catch the vision. They often won't even whisper about it until the key leaders of the church raise the possibilities. Romans 10:15 says, "And how shall they preach except they be sent?" That remains the responsibility of the local church, not only in terms of foreign missions, but right here at home as well.

V. The Principle of Giving

The Scriptures clearly reveal an eternal principle summed up in Luke 6:38. "Give, and it shall be given unto you; good measure, pressed down, and shaken together, and running over, shall men give into your bosom. For with the same measure that ye mete withal, it shall be measured to you again."

This verse is frequently and almost exclusively applied to individual giving. People are told, "You cannot out give the Lord." As evangelicals we believe this principle, but the verse has a wider connotation. It can apply to churches as well as individuals. A giving church is a growing church. This verse supports the view that churches that are willing to give some of their flock to establish new churches will themselves be blessed. Churches who do not respond when there is an evident need for establishing daughter churches often find themselves experiencing minimum growth and frequently find that other churches have begun in spite of them. Consequently, instead of having a daughter church, there is a church begun by another group or denomination. How much more satisfying it would be to commission a core group from the mother church to reach out into this new area for Christ.

No church has ever suffered, in the long run, from giving members to begin a daughter church. Testimonies are numerous of blessings received when a group of people have been "hived off" to establish a new work. Rather than the mother church suffering, there has been an influx of new people and a new excitement in both churches. Mature pastors are more interested in the total work of God than in their own local church. Jesus sums it up in these words recorded in Matthew "Freely ye have received, freely give."

VI. The Principle of Faith

When Paul was writing to the Corinthian believers about the future life, he threw them a curve when he inserted the phrase, "For we walk by faith, not by sight" (II Corinthians 5:7). Our goal is to be at home with the Lord permanently in heaven, but we are not there yet! In the meantime we are compelled by the love of Christ to share in His ministry of reconciliation.

But it is human nature to walk by sight! Many pastors walk by sight. They watch the attendance board, the church budget, the membership roll. Thoughts like these flow through their minds: "If I release some of my key workers, who would I get to replace them?" "If all those good tithers leave the church, my salary might be in jeopardy." "If those people leave, we might not reach our goals for this year." Everyone must deal with the real culprit — pride. Walking by sight displeases the Lord. After all, it is His work, not ours! He is the head of the church.

Establishing a daughter church demands great faith. But taking the challenge to exercise our faith makes Christian ministry exciting. Hebrews 11:6 reminds that without faith it is impossible to please God. Jesus told Peter to launch out into the deep. Deep water can be dangerous and risky, but that is where the greatest fishing is done.

VII. The Principle of Imitation

We tend to criticize people and churches when they imitate others. But while there are abuses, the imitation of good examples is a Biblical concept. In I Thessalonians 1:6, Paul commends the believers as he says, "And ye became followers (N.I.V. 'imitators') of us, and of the Lord ..." He further states in I Thessalonians 2:14, "For ye, brethren, became followers of the churches of God which in Judea are in Christ Jesus ..." There is the need for churches to imitate other model churches. But in our day, even more strikingly is there the need for better models to follow.

Without taking excursions into ego-bolstering, we need to take up the challenge in our churches of becoming those models. We need to acknowledge our responsibility to those who will follow us in this generation in our own community and elsewhere. Others are looking to us for models.

If this notion of starting daughter churches is a good idea for our day, we need to do it; in some cases not so much because our church has a pressing need to do it, as that other churches need to see it done successfully to spark their own initiative. How we praise God that this means of church growth has been used successfully in many places across the land. There are mother churches, large and small. There are very successful daughter churches. But still there is the need for more. Who will do it? Someone else, or you?

Admittedly our modern age is more complex than the first century, and therefore the exact methodology of doing God's work must be crafted to meet the needs of the current generation. But the principles of the Bible work in any generation. If the Apostle Paul were with us today, how would he approach the demands of our age? Would he be willing to maintain the present status quo? We know he was committed to the aggressive spreading of the gospel. He believed and lived out the great commission. He encouraged others to share their faith with the lost and to become missionary minded in their own world. He brought many spiritual babies into the world and taught them to reproduce. He sent them out. He consistently gave up his own rights, sacrificed and risked his very life as he stretched his own life of faith. Shouldn't we? Is it such a sacrifice to encourage the people in our churches to reproduce churches? We can be confident that Paul would actively endorse any method of growing a new church. He would be excited about your church making plans to establish a daughter church!

3

Problems or Possibilities?

The daughter church concept is often dismissed before it is given a thorough hearing. To many, it is a completely new idea, and to adopt it requires a radical change in thinking. So the opportunity is often ignored or rationalized out of a priority position, and the potential is left unrealized. Often the arguments used to down play the daughter church alternative are overstated, and positive answers to these negative attitudes are never really thought through.

All of the potential problems can be placed in one of three categories. Admittedly, some value judgment must be applied in categorizing a given problem.

Supposed Problems

Those not based in reality, but only in our thoughts and prejudices.

1. The community is not large enough to support another church.

Interestingly, one hears this statement made about communities of almost every size. While it may be true of some isolated villages, there usually are, even in these cases, sizeable towns or villages only a few miles away which need a solid evangelical testimony. With the increasing urbanization of our society, there will continue to be a great need for new churches established in our growing cities. Yet our larger cities and especially downtown core areas remain an untapped resource for church planting.

The fact is that as long as there are lost people in sufficient numbers, a community can support another work. If we think in terms of winning only five percent of the population in a community, very often the number will exceed the projected attendance of all the evangelical churches presently in that community. But who would argue that we should be satisfied without a concerted effort to reach them?

2. Our church isn't big enough to start a daughter church.

Nearly all churches seem to perceive the ideal size for mothering as one category larger than they presently are.

We all know there is more growing to be done in our own churches. But even a novice gardener also knows that at times you encourage a tree's growth by pruning it. The secret is deciding when and how to prune productively. If we don't prune our churches for growth at the proper time, one of two things is bound to happen: (1) stagnation will set in or (2) accidental pruning will occur. Accidental pruning happens when a group splits off or when people simply "die on the vine."

Thus, when a church has not seen recent growth, it may be a signal that it is time to prune — by planting a daughter church. Such a move is likely to stimulate the church to new heights by breaking in on established relationships and patterns in a positive way. Growth will be spurred again by the recent memories of how the sanctuary used to be full. Everyone will know that these pews are now empty because the church selflessly gave people to the daughter church. A holy dissatisfaction will engender enthusiasm to fill those places once again. History proves that this tends to occur in less than two years. The new found momentum may take the mother church to that next plateau that previously seemed out of reach.

3. We already have a worker shortage.

Especially in large churches, pleas for more workers tend to fall on deaf ears because people believe there must be "somebody out there" who can do "it" better than they can. All this is swept aside, however, when necessity hits both the mother and daughter churches. Talents hitherto buried are dug up and invested. Though the competence level may suffer temporarily, in service-training can quickly remedy that. Worker training may include the usual and often effective round of teacher training courses. Once the planning for the daughter church is well underway, a solid promotional thrust in this area will be well received by a surprising number of new workers.

If a mother church is planning ahead, it can duplicate the skills needed to serve in the roles of deacon, treasurer and such offices as are required to direct and manage church affairs. It must be borne in mind that new board or committee members usually learn the inner workings of their roles by working alongside others in the management group who have more experience. Care should be taken that decision making bodies, both in the parent and daughter church, still have a healthy contingent of experienced people to provide stability. In the event that this is not provided for, the pastor will be called upon more heavily to share his experience and insight.

4. Too many people may leave to form the daughter church.

When it comes right down to it, deciding to leave your home church is more difficult than most people suppose. The opposite is more generally the case. Everyone may be for the idea of the daughter work so long as they may simply pray and give. Going isn't what most have in mind; the ties are just too strong. Only a committed, motivated nucleus can make a new church succeed.

5. The daughter church will be too close to the mother.

The distance between church locations is seldom a deciding factor in the choice of a church home. While the location of a church is important in establishing overall appeal and identification in the community, people will regularly drive past one church to go to another. The reason is that churches are not built primarily on geographical relationships; they are built on personal relationships. Research has indicated that at least eighty-five percent of people who attend a given church for the first time do so because they are invited by a friend, a neighbour or a relative. As relationships begin to develop within the daughter church, people do not see the old friends from the parent church as often. The simple reason is that time is now used in maintaining and developing contacts within the new church community.

Looking at this supposed problem from this perspective soon reveals that however close the two churches may be geographically, once the daughter church is firmly established another kind of distance will develop — a social distance. This is not unhealthy. It is merely to be expected as one of the natural results of having two separate churches.

The only church goers I know who highly value proximity to their church are senior citizens who tend to be less mobile. The rest of us make choices for complex reasons that have little to do with geography. Generally speaking, people will not feel a sense of belonging to a church merely because they live in the area of the church.

Potential Problems

Those real problems that may occur but don't need to.

1. Misunderstanding in the new community

This surfaces in the question, "Why are you starting a new church when there are so many in town which are almost empty?" To such persons, evangelism equals proselytism, which is widely frowned upon in our society. If the planned expansion programme is properly presented in literature for both churches, and in the attitudes and statements of the people of both churches, the problem can be virtually eliminated.

People in both the mother and daughter churches must be carefully trained to answer this question from a biblical perspective. The following analogy may be helpful. "Suppose you were driving down a dark road at night and a kilometer ahead there was an unmarked collapsed bridge. If I were parked at the side of the road and watched car after car go by, including yours, you would think me a fool or criminally negligent. On the other hand, if I jumped out in front of you and made you come to a screeching halt, you would initially be annoyed with me.

"After I explained about the bridge, you still might not believe me and drive on regardless, but I would have fulfilled my responsibility to you. I'd feel terrible about your decision, but I wouldn't feel guilty.

"Our church believes that men and women really are headed for a fallen bridge called Judgement Day, and we'd like to do everything we can to forestall disaster. Not everyone will believe what we say, of course, but we must not be silent. Establishing this new church is like putting up one more 'Bridge Out' sign."

2. Mistrust between the mother and daughter congregations

It is inevitable that the two congregations will develop different styles of ministry as they go along. If they agree from the outset that the daughter church is not expected to be a carbon copy, both can handle the divergence smoothly and even view it with pleasure. Unfortunately, in some cases, pent up differences explode in the formation of a new church. In these less than ideal situations, there is a tendency to overreaction. Principles held dear in the mother church are left unrespected in the ill-timed daughter. Such unhealthy scenarios can usually be avoided, however. There simply must be an open fellowship at the pastoral level of the two churches. This warmth can then permeate both congregations. Interchurch functions may also be desirable. The two boards can meet for an hour or two quarterly to keep each other up to date.

3. Screening leadership candidates in the daughter church

As soon as the new church is established, people seem to "come out of the woodwork." These often appear to be excellent but sometimes prove to be a disappointment. New churches tend to attract the dispossessed, the misfits looking for a place in the sun, those who have been denied significant roles in other churches.

There is always the chance, of course, that they may become willing and capable workers in this new setting. If they are truly born again, we must not despise or ignore them. Their needs, in fact, are a powerful argument in favour of starting new churches that will minister to them. But we must also exercise discernment in finding roles appropriate for them. Their needs must be met, but the need of the new church for stable leadership takes precedence.

Failure in new churches is often attributable to bad judgment and hasty decisions made by people who have been thrust into leadership roles before they developed sufficient spiritual maturity and knowledge to handle difficult decisions. The daughter church concept, when properly applied, eliminates much of this problem by transplanting trusted, mature leaders of like mind and doctrine at the outset. This benefit saves years in the life of the daughter church.

Real Problems

Problems in church mothering that may well be universal.

1. Imperfect attitudes

When one deals with deep questions relating to one's church home; the issues become very personal. The daughter church idea challenges a church at the deepest levels. It means rending the fabric of church life. Even though the tearing apart is productive, the warp and woof of the church life involved is radically stretched and torn. It is much like sending a favorite child off to college, or moving to a new community. It is also like the pain of childbirth. All of these are part of life. But all are uncomfortable.

Some will not handle these strains well. Christian grace must be carefully applied at each step along the road to establishing a daughter church.

In the conceptual stage, from the first time the idea of a daughter church is mentioned, everyone involved must begin guarding his or her attitudes and motives as well as the tongue. The idea must be introduced in a most wholesome context. For example, starting a daughter church to eliminate a personality conflict will only bury a problem which will eventually reemerge. Solve any such difficulties first and then start talking about a daughter church.

In the planning stage, each participant must be selfless in his contributions to the discussion.

In the presentation stage, clarity is essential. Carefully chosen words and visuals are necessary to keep small misunderstandings from swelling. People must be encouraged to ask their questions of someone who has a knowledgeable answer. Board members must have the facts exactly correct and be able to communicate with them. The questions, "Why are we doing this?" "Is this a cover up?" may not be verbalized, but some will be thinking them. So answer them.

Once the new church gets underway people must recognize that not everyone will be involved in the decision-making meetings of both churches. Some who have always been in on major decisions in their church may feel awkward about this. There is a sense of loss of control. Therefore, be careful to spell out what is happening, and never attribute bad motives to an action you don't understand. Love believes, bears, hopes and endures all things.

In the ongoing stages, maintain positive love between the congregations. The two churches are not in competition for members; that is totally unbiblical. Over time, most members will wind up talking with someone who is struggling over whether to go or stay. These discussions need to proceed as objectively as possible without coercion or obscuring of the relative facts. Both churches will not be the same, and people will choose one or the other for reasons which are highly individual. Probably a small shift of membership will occur back and forth between the churches for a variety of reasons. This shift is inevitable and really only points to the fact that the variety inherent in two different options is a desirable situation to provide ministry to different types of people.

2. Downscaling

Nearly every part of the daughter church suffers by comparison with its mother. Families have to give up closely graded Christian education, for example. The boy who was used to a full class of third graders is now in a mixed class for grades one through three that includes, perish the thought, his younger sister! Neither of them may be too sure about that idea at first. And yet the only solution to such difficulties is growth, which will take a few years.

What about midweek programming? The daughter church that tries to duplicate the mother's array of youth clubs will tax its good workers severely.

Music is another valued area which won't be the same. Fewer pianists will be available, but it still takes one to play for every service. There will probably be no organ, or an inferior one, and a smaller choir if any.

The same situations are repeated in other areas. Probably the area which will cause many families to stay with the mother church is the ministry to teens. Few high schoolers want to give up a youth group of thirty or forty for a group that can't even field a mixed softball team. And yet, after all is said and done and the dust has settled after the turbulent teen years, what do we find? Smaller churches seem to produce godly adults and especially Christian leaders beyond all proportion to their size. Maybe the smaller church isn't so deprived after all. We need to challenge parents with this fact.

In planning the programming for the daughter church, duplication of the ministries of the mother church is not possible. A type of strategic withdrawal of leadership and resources is essential to survival. With all the new patterns to be set, it will be necessary to carefully choose some areas for planned neglect.

Consideration of these problems should be given by the mother church so that some support is available in the areas chosen for planned neglect. For example, perhaps the children from the daughter church would still be welcome in the midweek program of the mother church if the daughter opts to forego the development of its own for the first year.

In every case where resources of the mother church must be drawn upon, the goal should be that such reliance will be of minimum extent and duration. If leaning on the mother church becomes a comfortable posture, the daughter will not develop its own muscles. In such an event, a frank discussion initiated by the mother may be in order.

3. Money

Launching a daughter church should probably be the major ministry expansion of the year for the mother church. Besides helping with operating costs, the mother church should be heavily involved in the daughter's building fund. Many suggest that providing the land for the daughter's building is a realistic project.

Meanwhile, the daughter church will find that its budget proportions look very different from what has been the norm in the mother church. The pastor's salary takes a greater percentage than before. This must be accepted, not resented; it is normal. And the pastor must not feel guilty. Another area where the percentage rises is promotion. A lot of paper will be bought and used. Duplicating equipment must be purchased if not borrowed from the mother church.

In light of such immediate needs, is there room for missions giving? The fledgling church will not be able to give much; indeed, it is a mission itself. But supporting missions in some way still makes sense because it creates a base that can grow over the years.

All of these problems can be viewed as challenges and opportunities. Some solutions are still waiting to be discovered. The combination of creativity, hard work and faith in a big God will carry venturesome churches far in their quest.

We have seen that there are few, if any, insurmountable problems for the church that has the will to succeed in church mothering. However, an unidentified uncertainty about the idea may still linger in the minds of some. That hesitation may stem from wondering whether or not the church is ready for such an ambitious undertaking. A church and its pastor want to know that such a challenge is one which they ought to face. The following evaluative questions may help crystallize thinking at both the congregational and pastoral level. Sometimes the feelings of hesitation are rooted in fear. We all want to be sure we don't "bury talents" because of fear.

Questions for the Local Congregation

1. Are we spiritually and emotionally prepared, able to carry the stress, planning and care of a new work?

Prayer is an essential ingredient in the establishing of a daughter church. If there is frequent public and private prayer among the members of the church concerning the matter, that is a good sign of the readiness of the people. Frequent reminders to pray about the matter are essential.

Most churches feel, at some points of time and in certain facets of their ministry, that they are barely able to survive. Careful thought needs to be given to the mother church's perception of itself. The church needs to believe that it is strong enough to handle the task of parenting at the present time. That, of course, does not mean that the church believes it is without weak spots. It simply means that there is a general sense of health in the midst of the normal aches and pains of ministry.

A mother church needs to have sufficient resources to provide some element of parental example, stability and protection. That probably means that the mother church must not have had any sort of "bumpy roads" in its recent past.

2. Are we financially capable of carrying such a project?

Financial assistance is needed in a new work. We are admonished by our Lord that he who builds a house must count the cost (Luke 14:28-30). There are increased costs from the beginning of a daughter church project. When you start with the same number of people, simply divided into two groups, it is obvious that there is a need for greater giving from people on both sides of the mother/daughter team.

Careful analysis and budget preparation will enable you to predict expenses related to the new church, but you must agree as a group of individuals to handle these additional expenses with increased giving.

3. Are we willing to support the new congregation in every possible way?

Support may well go beyond the financial. A mother church must be willing to loan out equipment when necessary for the daughter's use. This may mean that a Sunday school teacher will be asked to give up a favorite table for some time while it is on loan. Perhaps that separate set of hymn books the choir uses from time to time will be needed by the daughter church. You see, there may be some slight deprivations required to make the idea work. The daughter needs to know that if she asks for help it will not be withheld or grudgingly given. There are all sorts of ways in which the mother can help. She ought to be overjoyed to share things like duplicating equipment, chairs, office space, and even workers.

Questions for the Pastor

1. Can I bear the pressures of losing effective church leadership?

The most difficult part of the project for the pastor of a mother church is the loss of members. This is particularly acute when leaders move out from the mother church to be a part of the daughter. Sometimes pastors, in their own insecurities, cannot get free of the irrational emotions that cause them to feel rejected by those who have moved on to the new work. It makes no difference how much these daughter church people assure him of their love and support. He may accept their statements in his mind and still feel hurt in his heart. Such emotions go beyond the normal sense of loss when loved people move away to a new community.

2. Can I cope with seeing numerical losses?

In a growth and success oriented world, numbers are seen as the symbols of success. In terms of what will happen in the confines of the four walls of the mother church, there will be a temporary dip in the attendance and offering figures. This may be hardest for the pastor to take. He may become a little defensive and fearful that things won't rebound. If the rebound is not fast enough for him, this, too, will be difficult. Usually within a year or so things will be back to the same levels as before the parenting endeavour. In some cases, there is no perceivable lag whatsoever. Perhaps, then, the real question is, "Can I cope with the fear of seeing numerical losses?" The fear may be far worse than the reality.

3. Can I cope with the success of the daughter church?

A pastor must decide that he will not be threatened by the success of the new church. If they require the use of the mother church's baptistry and baptize more than the mother church, that should be a source of genuine rejoicing and not seen as some sort of failure in a competition. Both churches are on the same team, not on opposing sides!

It will test the spiritual mettle of the mother church's pastor if the pastor of the daughter church appears to be more successful or effective in some elements of ministry. An especially sensitive area is preaching ability.

4. Can I cope if the new church does not work out as expected?

As much as success can be threatening for the pastor of the mother church, failure or the fear of it is often an equal threat. The pastor of the mother church will need to bite his tongue often as decisions are made that he might not personally prefer. As the personality and style of the new church evolves, it will become increasingly apparent that the daughter is not a clone of the mother. This might prove a little embarrassing if the mother church's pastor is more rigid in his thinking, and especially if he has stated strong personal preferences as if they were convictions, only to find that the daughter walks away from some of those preferences.

5. Can I take the strain of sharing limited resources on a short term basis?

The need for sharing various resources may cause some inconvenience. This could become a source of irritation in the heart of the mother church's pastor. He already has enough interruptions in his day and enough unexpected difficulties to sort out. It takes a deep commitment to the parent/daughter concept to enable one to forge ahead with a positive heart.

In all of the deliberation and introspection, one must be assured that the course being contemplated is the one which will maximize real impact for the Lord and the growth of His enterprise — the church. Each man must be revived in his spirit and totally transparent with himself. It is sometimes easy for a man to mask his own agenda and goals with statements concerning God's will and God's timing. A spiritual man is truly in tune with his Master. Be that man, and you will make wise choices regarding the daughter church possibility.

The article which forms the basis for this chapter was first published in LEADERSHIP, Winter, 1985.

4

Is There a Procedure That Works?

The idea of establishing daughter churches carries many different emotional loads for people. To some the idea simply seems strange. To others it appears to be a euphemism for "church split." To still others, the idea is great — but only for some other church! Because of this, it is important to follow a well thought out procedure when discussing the subject with those who may not have the same starting point as yourself.

We suggest here a framework within which anyone may work who wishes to see God work in the establishment of a daughter church, particularly a pastor. Because of the individuality of each situation, few time goals are stated. There is a five-phase procedure. We encourage you to project how long the various phases might take in your own situation. Attach a date to the projected time when you believe you could complete each phase given the particulars of your situation. You may even be prepared to call these projections goals!

Phase I: Inspiration

The purpose of this phase is to establish a positive mental attitude in the potential mother church toward the concept in general. The church needs to hear about success stories in other places. Particularly the pastor and the key leadership need to be aware of what God is doing in this kind of church planting. Reading material that is informative and inspirational is a good place to begin. Unfortunately, very little is available in a written form on this subject, even though there are many churches experiencing, first hand, the glow of this form of church planting.

Dean Merrill has written an informative article, "Mothering a New Church", published in the journal, Leadership (Winter 1985, pp. 98-104). It is built around a recent survey which indicated that of those who have been involved in church parenting, about eighty-five percent hoped there would be a next time as the Lord leads. That indicates positive experience indeed!

In this stage of inspiration there must be the development of a conviction in the hearts of the people that this type of church growth is a viable way to fulfill the great commission. Watch for it emerging among the people as they identify with reports of testimonies of what God is doing in other places.

The advantages and difficulties of this concept must be understood and assimilated into the thinking of the key leadership of the congregation with the resultant conviction that the advantages are well worth the price paid.

Phase II: Investigation

At this point in the procedure the goal is to collect data which will be used to awaken within the membership of the potential mother church a desire to consider the possibility of establishing a daughter church in their situation. The pastor needs to involve his trusted and best leaders in prayerful investigation of the available research data to develop a knowledge of the potential in their own environs. How many households are in a given area? What are the population projections? Is there major industrial expansion on the horizon? Is there a particular segment of the population on the rise (e.g. ethnic groups, seniors, students)? What about new highways, roads, sewers and subdivisions? This kind of information is usually available by making a few phone calls or visits to local government administrators. You will want to be aware if your church is likely to be ineffective in penetrating an area because it is separated by a highway, a river or a railway track which makes access difficult.

Take a good look at your own membership data. Are there significant numbers of people coming from a geographical area who might identify as a core group for a new church? Is there a group with an ethnic background that shows potential to reach its own kind of people if a separate church were formed? Is there any group of people whose needs could be better met by the formation of a new church? What about the growth limitations in the facilities in which you are now meeting? Do you realize that you will not consistently see your building used to any more than the eighty percent saturation point?

This investigative stage is so important. If you hear a question raised, do your best to find a satisfying answer. Turn over every stone, while all the time asking the Lord to make you aware of the information you need to make the right decisions.

Phase III: Information

This is probably the most crucial stage. The purpose is to obtain a commitment to look at the parent/daughter option in specifics. It is not the time to decide to go ahead with it. It is simply the time to develop a model of what you envisage in regard to a daughter church. As a tentative model begins to surface for a needed new congregation, work towards gaining official sanction to develop a detailed study and specific proposal. It is important that this model take careful consideration of the consensus of the congregation.

Work towards an information meeting for the entire congregation, at which time the daughter church proposal will be presented. It is best to plan to have a written report to hand out at this meeting. Bear in mind that not everyone will attend, yet all need the information.

This presentation should answer as many questions as possible. The people need to have help to be able to project themselves into the new situation after a new church is formed, whether they plan to join with the new work or stay with the mother church.

The detailed information should describe the daughter church proposal in one of three general categories or streams as seems most appropriate based on research and prayer.

Stream 1: Brisk Flow

In this case the daughter church would be designed to be completely indigenous from the beginning, with the minimum of dependence on the mother church. This approach has the fewest difficulties for the new church; but, of course, it is the most expensive for the mother church. It is expensive not only in terms of money, but also in terms of loss of manpower. Perhaps the most costly area is in the loss of control over the decision making of the daughter church. It frustrates the impulses of mother when daughter changes the status quo and does the unexpected. When that divergence of opinion is handled right, it can be a great source of maturity for the mother church; she must learn to let go — after all, a Baptist church is autonomous! And, of course, it will be maturing for the daughter church to learn from its own mistakes.

If this stream is chosen, the start up period is fast, neat and clean. It may be a little traumatic, but at least the pain of severing close working relationships is dealt with quickly. The inevitable differences which will emerge quickly between the two churches underscore the need of the mother church to be galvanized by frequent reminders that the daughter will not be a clone of the mother.

There are various implications to this "brisk flow" stream which should be mentioned. There must, of course, be a sufficient number of motivated people, including enough wage earners leaving from the mother church to enable the new church to handle all its own expenses. There will need to be enough workers enlisted to handle as full a slate of programmes as possible without overtaxing any individuals or sapping strength from the needed aggressive outreach program.

Temporary meeting quarters for the daughter church should be arranged. It is best to acquire a place that can be used for midweek programmes as well as Sundays. This place should be big enough to handle space requirements until a permanent location is obtained. If the church must move from one temporary location to another it not only complicates things for the church people, but to some watching from the community it will project an aura of instability.

The best approach seems to be to have a full-time pastor ready to take the oversight at the very beginning. This means that before people leave the mother church for the uncertainties of the daughter church, they are aware of the personality, vision, gifts and style of the key leader around which the new church will take shape. It may be possible to take the daughter church's pastor on to the staff of the mother church for a while to help establish a rapport and good working relationship in advance.

The major contribution the mother church will make to the financial success of the new work is the giving up of many, probably at least twenty tithing families. In addition, consideration should be given by the mother church to making a major contribution to the daughter church towards their building programme. Often this could take the form of accepting financial responsibility for the land expense.

Circumstances vary, but it is realistic to expect that if this "brisk flow" stream is followed, the daughter church will be in possession of a permanent building within a two to five year period.

Stream 2: Moderate Flow

In this case, the daughter church would be phased into an indigenous position over a period of a few years. To start with, there would probably be a separate Sunday morning service and Sunday school; but there may be a shared evening service, shared midweek children's programming and a shared youth group. In addition, there may be some interplay on the decision making level with a representative from the mother church sitting on the board of the daughter church.

The need for founding members will not be quite as great as in the case of a "brisk flow" stream. But there will be similar needs for facilities. Even if there is no need for midweek programming locations to start, there must be some consideration given to this element if midweek programming is expected to be in operation before the possession of permanent facilities.

The budget may call for a part time or "tent making" pastor. Otherwise substantial support will be needed from the mother church, or will need to be raised through the Home Mission Board or otherwise from churches in the association or from individuals. But it still seems best, not to say essential, to have the founding pastor in place from the outset.

The mother church will have longer term financial responsibility to the daughter church. The same building and land considerations should apply as in the "brisk flow" approach.

It is reasonable to project that this type of daughter church will be in possession of its own building in a period of three to seven years, but there will probably continue to be a need for financial support from outside of the daughter congregation during this period and in some cases longer.

Stream 3: Gentle Flow

In this type of situation the daughter church usually evolves out of a prayer meeting established with a few concerned families. It may even be the evidence of a strategy by a potential mother church to establish a "shepherding" group in a given area with the hope and expectation that it will grow into a full-fledged church.

Probably this prayer meeting will proceed for a year or two without the concept of a new church being high profile in the group members' hearts or in their meetings. The new church concept may be more of a secret ideal cherished by the leadership.

In cases where there are not larger population centres, or where the potential mother church itself is not that strong, this may be the most appropriate stream. Even in cases where the mother church is larger, but perhaps not entirely sympathetic for a variety of reasons, this type of group, sanctioned by the leadership of the potential mother church, may form the nucleus of a church that will actually take shape in future years.

When the group has grown to a size where it is ready to establish some independence, a final thrust of help from the mother church may be all that is needed to form the desired new church.

Leadership for this kind of group may be provided by a layman, a former vocational Christian worker or a theological student. Stable leadership is important so that steps of expansion are planned and undertaken in such a way that the group does not overextend itself and have to back track. Such backward steps undermine the confidence of the community; and that confidence is hard to regain.

If this "gentle flow" stream is followed, it may not be as necessary to involve the entire congregation in a high profile presentation as it is in the other two streams.

The choice of stream for the formation of a daughter church in a given situation will depend upon many factors. Here are some you will want to consider:

1. The potential of the field

In the geographical area you service, what percentage of the population could you believe God wants saved and in a church of like faith to your own?

How many churches will it take to service these people? How long will it take to plant that number of churches? When should the next one be started?

2. The potential of your church

Do the people really care about fulfilling the great commission here at home? Do they believe God wants to bless in this way? Is there sufficient potential leadership? Is the mood and climate of the church such that they could rise to the challenge of significant sacrifice of money and manpower?

3. The potential of the pastor

Does he have the confidence of the people to lead them in this kind of endeavour at this time? Does he have a vision broader than the ministry of one church? Would it be too difficult for him to live with the pressures involved?

The analysis of these factors is somewhat subjective. Such consideration will reflect the mindset of the analyzer with regard to daughter churches. If he truly believes in the idea, he will tend to see more potential.

Let me encourage your vision with some observations. There are tremendous benefits to making the fastest start possible. Since it is more blessed to give than to receive, when a mother church really stretches, she reaps the greatest benefit. The natural tendency seems to be to achieve the formation of the daughter church with the least possible disruption to the mother church.

This is an effort to reduce the pain of separation that is inherent in the concept. But if the formation of the new church grinds on slowly, two things will inevitably happen. First, the new ministry is likely to occupy a very small part of the awareness, and thus the prayers of the people. It is rather like having a lot of lead time for preparation of a college term paper. Few in the class think about it much until the deadline approaches. While people ought to be shaping their own phase of ministry to accommodate the changes necessary when the new church starts, they probably won't.

Second, if the daughter church is projected to come into existence over a longer period of time, those who are most enthusiastic about the idea must deal with a high level of frustration while they cool their heels waiting for something to happen.

In summary, may I suggest you choose your course of action carefully. The fastest stream possible in the circumstances is the best. Make your presentation as pleasing and complete as possible. This "Information" phase material must answer the questions people will ask: What will this do to us as a church? Who will the new pastor be or how will he be selected? Where will the daughter church meet? Will there be enough programming and fellowship to meet the needs of all my family members? Think of what people will want to know and give them satisfying answers.

When the needs are clearly understood and the daughter church model is designed to meet the needs in the particular case, there should be strong support of the model from the board of the mother church. With a model designed from one of the three streams, it should be relatively easy to obtain support for some form of daughter church if the pastor and key leaders are united on the basis of their own investigations.

Phase IV: Intention

This is the phase where actual decisions are made. Having designed the model or approach, then having fine tuned it according to the feedback from your people, it is time to leave the realm of the theoretical and make some decisions. The priority and urgency of these specific decisions will, of course, depend on the stream to be followed. But the decisions listed here must be made at some point in time. Some overlapping may occur amongst Phases III, IV and V. It is wise to postpone decisions if doing so leaves the daughter church in a stronger position to shape its own destiny under God.

Decisions to be made:
1. Board approval of the daughter church model including the setting of a timetable for implementation.
2. Congregational approval of the model.

3. Calling of a pastor for the daughter church.
4. Temporary meeting place established and furniture acquired.
5. Land purchase or the purchase of an option to purchase (preferred).
6. Individual family decisions to join the daughter church — signing of commitment forms.
7. Name for the daughter church.
8. Preliminary budget approval.
9. Support responsibilities of the mother church specified.
10. Date and plans for a commissioning service.
11. Publicity plans for both mother and daughter to affirm continued support of one another.
12. Election and appointment of workers in the daughter church and the replacements required in the mother church.

Phase V: Inception

In this phase the daughter church has developed a separate identity and is working toward the organization of itself as a duly constituted church. This would be followed by an appropriate recognition service.

Of course, it goes beyond the scope of this material to present suggestions for organizing and building a church. But if the leadership people of the church are resourceful, they will find a host of ideas to implement in the life of the church. At this stage of its development the scope of opportunity is broad. No one can say, "We've never done it that way before!" The church has never done anything before! This period of time presents the opportunity to try some new ideas without becoming too trendy or leaving the solid foundations.

Special attention must be given to the outreach of the church. It is advisable to plan to neglect some of the least effective ministries the people may have been used to in order to concentrate resources on community penetration.

Time is short, the task is urgent, the possibilities of faith are limitless. These are reminders all of us need, and often. Here is a procedure for church planting that can revitalize your own church. How will you respond to the questions: If not here ... where? If not now ... when? If not me ... who? God help us to accept the challenge.

5

What About Those Prototypes?

When the apostle Paul commended the church at Philippi for their generosity in supporting him in the ministry of church planting, he was referring to tangible support. Such support is a necessity if the work of starting new churches is to increase. However, more than financial resources are needed. Established churches must be challenged to commission a group of members to branch out and open a new work. Some call such churches daughters, some branch churches, others extension works or even sister churches. Whatever the title, the concept is the same.

We should say at the outset that this type of church extension does not in any way minimize the important place of large churches. There is a real need for large churches in Canada today. What would Victoria be without Central Baptist Church, or Saskatoon without Circle Alliance Church? Queensway Cathedral in Toronto, now seating over three thousand, is exercising considerable influence. The Peoples Church, Toronto, world renowned, continues to minister to multitudes. Super churches are carrying out a ministry that is unique and vital, and need not be superseded by the parent/daughter church concept. It is not a matter of having one without the other, but rather of having the two.

It is easy to come to the conclusion that starting a branch work will to some extent hinder the growth of the parent church and slow its development. This is seldom so. In the vast majority of cases, starting a daughter work does not curtail the growth of the parent church.

We would do well to revive the practice of starting daughter churches that was so evident at the turn of the century in North America. In 1901, a great minister was called to serve the historic First Presbyterian Church of Seattle, Washington. He accepted the challenge, provided the church would agree to start daughter churches. That church was ultimately responsible for planting thirty-five churches in the greater Seattle area.

Southern Baptist churches have long been in the forefront in this method of church reproduction. Thousands of their churches have been responsible for branch works. Walnut Street Baptist Church, Louisville, Kentucky is known as the "First Baptist Church" of that city. Over the course of its lifetime, it has been instrumental in starting twenty-six other churches.

In the late 1970s, a survey was taken of the forty Fellowship Baptist churches in Toronto. Over half had been started from a parent church.

When Ron Kernohan became pastor of Brantview Baptist Church, Calgary, he set his sights on starting a daughter church within a five year period. He laid the groundwork through pulpit ministry, encouraging his officers and setting goals together. The church caught the vision of the pastor and made it their objective too. They made the initial step of purchasing an excellent site near the university. A year before the extension work was to start, an extension pastor was called. His job description was to teach an adult Bible class made up of members who would form the nucleus of the daughter work. His visitation focused on the target community. It was a memorable Sunday in September, 1982, when the church commissioned fifty members to start their daughter work. They were some of the leading members and officers, including the chairman of the deacons, the church treasurer and the Sunday School superintendent, and they were encouraged to leave by their pastor, himself!

North Park Bible Chapel in London, Ontario, under the leadership of their teaching elder, Dr. William McRae, observed that a large number of families were coming from the extreme west side of the city. He led in securing a building in the heart of west London. Today the new work has taken off and is planning to build, while the main work has continued to grow and develop. Continuing in faith, the main chapel has now started a second branch work.

The experience of the Scarborough Gospel Temple in Toronto is an exciting and stirring example of what can be done in terms of church reproduction right across America. Pastor Hudson Hilsden, who is now Coordinator of Social Concern and Public Relations for the Pentecostal Assemblies of Canada, was called to serve Scarborough Gospel Temple in 1975. When the board of the church interviewed him initially, they asked how he looked upon church reproduction. He heartily concurred that this was a ministry of the local church.

Within his first year the church commissioned thirty-one members, including some of the important leaders of the church, to start the Markham Pentecostal Church. This church is located about fifteen miles away in a major developing community of greater Toronto. The church also provided a $5,000 down payment towards the purchase of a ten-acre site. This laid the groundwork for the new church and gave it visibility in Markham.

The Sunday after the group left, the church did not notice any decrease in attendance or offerings. This served to encourage the congregation to consider another opportunity. The Inter Church Planning Association (an organization of over fifteen denominations in Canada, established to help churches purchase property) made available to the Pentecostal Assemblies a choice three-acre site at Sheppard and Neilson in Scarborough. Scarborough Gospel Temple took up the challenge and put down a payment of $37,000 towards the total price of $150,000. The provision was that the church had five years in which to build on the property. The congregation voted ninety-six percent in favour of starting a new church. Little did the church anticipate that over the space of seven years a total of $260,000 would be given to get that new church off to a glorious start.

A five-year plan was agreed upon. Assistant Pastor Dave Imler was to start a Sunday School the first year. In year two, morning services would be held with united evening services in the parent church. In year three, evening services got underway. Rev. Donald Feltmate, then Executive Director of Church Ministries for the Pentecostal Assemblies, responded to the call of the new church which was now composed of one hundred members and adherents from the parent body. Year four was design year, when the edifice was planned, and year five was building year. It is interesting to note that the time schedule agreed upon was followed to the letter. Today this $850,000 building has from six to seven hundred people in attendance in a church that is only eight years old.

It should also be noted that the new work is only three miles away from the parent church, yet it did not affect adversely the attendance or the offerings of the parent work. Today there are two churches of almost equal size cooperating together, where less than a decade ago there was only one. This gives evidence of mature leadership and a selfless spirit on the part of pastors and people.

There are basically eight models or types of daughter churches. Each one has its advantages, and none is superior to the others. Each local church has its own character and therefore must adopt the model best suited to its needs and structure.

1. Pastor led daughter churches

These are, as the title implies, churches that are started under the leadership of a pastor. It is the pastor who sees the need of a particular community and sets out to plant a church there. He prayerfully presents this to his people, and by his teaching and influence gradually leads his congregation to take up the challenge.

Rev. Godfrey Catanus was born, raised and educated in the Philippines. When he moved to Canada he saw thousands of his own people residing in Toronto. After planting the first Filipino Baptist church in Canada there, he moved to British Columbia and proceeded to start a second new church. Now he is back in Toronto, in his third church planting experience.

Godfrey's brother, Eliezer, immigrated to Canada with the same spirit. Succeeding his brother in Toronto, he took up the pastorate with a specific goal of seeing two new churches started, one on the east and one on the west side, since the original church is centrally located. As the auditorium was filling to capacity, he came to the conclusion that he would rather have three churches in three different parts of the city than one large centralized church. He holds the conviction that three pastors working in three areas will have a greater impact than will three pastors working out of the one centre.

Faith Baptist Church, St. Thomas, Ont., had the privilege of having their senior pastor, Rev. Donald Fitchett, and his assistant, the coauthor of this book, Rev. Gary Carter, share the same vision: namely to plant a daughter church in the eastern part of the city. Although that work is only a little over two miles from the parent church, both churches are now growing and flourishing.

Rev. Harold Duckworth had a fruitful ministry at First Baptist Church, Kamloops, B.C. Seeing two outlying areas of the city without a meaningful gospel witness, he began a daughter church program. Under his leadership the Dallas-Barnhartvale Church got underway on the extreme eastern edge of the city. Five years later he led in the commencement of Westsyde Baptist Church, on the other side of Kamloops.

Blessed is the church whose pastor is willing to start a daughter work. Doubly blessed is the church who has in succession two pastors with the same vision. Such has been the case with First Baptist Church, Lloydminster, SK.

Early in 1976, Ken Roach, a deacon at the Lloydminster church travelled thirty-six miles to Vermilion, Alberta, each Friday night to lead family

Bible study hour. Opening sessions were held in the home of Mr. and Mrs. Dale Hollen who had been converted a year earlier under the ministry of Pastor Vern Priebe of the Lloydminster church. Pastor Priebe and the deacons encouraged the Hollens to start a church. Before long there was a solid development. The local Plymouth Brethren Assembly closed and turned their assets over to the new church. A call was extended to Mr. Ted Clark, who was at that time a chartered accountant in Hay River, North West Territories, to come to Vermilion as a tentmaker pastor. Services began on Sunday, September 6, 1976. Today the Vermilion church is able to support a full-time pastor and has erected a fine building to house its services.

We should mention that the Lloydminster church aided the Vermilion work in the purchase of property and in the erection of a building. This was accomplished at the same time that the parent church was erecting a new, much needed building to house its own growing congregation. The question was raised whether the church could build and assist a daughter work at the same time. Experience gave a resounding yes. Within two years the Lloydminster church had erected a one million dollar edifice, while at the same time giving generously to Vermilion.

Pastor Priebe moved to Vancouver and Harvey Peters followed him at Lloydminster. Like the people to whom he came, he, too, had a heart for church planting. This soon became evident when a new opportunity arose. In June 1980, the door opened to start a work in Maidstone, Saskatchewan, forty miles east of Lloydminster. Dick Thiessen and Wes Friesen, deacons, provided leadership in the early stages. A midweek service commenced on February 6, 1981, and Sunday services on November 23 of the same year. It was not long before Pastor Gordon Marchant and his wife Aleta moved to the community and took over leadership of the new church. Again the parent church showed a generous attitude toward its second child.

Has this effort hurt the Lloydminster church? Undoubtedly there has been a cost, not merely financial, but in time and effort, and in the giving of members for the task. But it has only enhanced the missionary heart of the

Lloydminster church and its other ministries have not suffered. Indeed, there is much to indicate that it has only made the church stronger and the testimony of Christ in the region more widespread.

An additional chapter to this story is the birth of the first grandchild of the Lloydminster church when in 1982 services got underway in Elk Point, Alberta. This is a daughter work of Vermilion under the leadership of Pastor John McGregor. It would appear that there are some genetic characteristics passed on in church planting, for the missionary heart of Vermilion and Maidstone is not unlike that of the parent church.

2. People led daughter churches

Again, as is obvious by the name, this is where a group of people within an established church are the ones who have a vision for starting a new work. These may be several families who live together in a certain area, or a group of people sensing a particular community where a church is needed. Usually, two or three families will share together this mutual vision, and will present it to their pastor.

Having his approval, a series of prayer meetings for the new work will be announced from the pulpit and those interested are encouraged to join together to prayerfully consider their participation. God can use this time to knit their hearts together, and the people will soon realize whether or not they should proceed with the founding of a daughter work.

This was the experience in the early 1970s, when several members of Elliott Heights Baptist Church, Hamilton, Ontario, saw the need of a new work about four miles from their church. After a series of prayer meetings, West Highland Baptist Church was formed and within a ten year period has become the largest of the Fellowship Baptist churches in the whole Hamilton and Niagara Region Association. Seven years later history repeated itself as four families of West Highland Baptist Church in the same fashion started a new church in neighbouring Ancaster. So the mantle of church growth is passed on through daughter works.

3. Association led daughter churches

Another common type of church planting occurs when a group of churches within close geographical boundaries work together to start a new church in an area mutually agreed upon. Churches with families in that particular community will encourage participation in the new church. Financial aid will usually be made available.

The strength of this method lies in the combined effort of several churches working together. Because a number of churches are involved, a greater motivation to succeed exists. Generally there are more families throughout an association who are willing to form the work. Also considerable prayer interest and support is generated as reports are made to the supporting churches. Often this interest will motivate others to join the enterprise to experience the excitement and thrill of being part of a new work.

Village Green Baptist Church, London, Ontario, was a project of the London and District Association of The Fellowship of Evangelical Baptist Churches in Canada. Members came from several of the churches, with Wortley Baptist providing the largest number of families. The entire project was covered financially by the churches, including pastoral support and purchase of land.

One disadvantage of this method is the natural difficulty of blending successfully families from different churches, each with its own identity and emphasis. Even churches of the same denomination, with a common doctrinal statement, will differ in form of worship, evangelism, ministries and outreach. This becomes a greater problem if the founding pastor is committed to the position of one particular group. It is important that an experienced pastor be sought with a track record of well-balanced ministry.

4. Association led churches with a denominational board

This is a combined effort, with churches of a given association working together with a national board to provide a solid footing for a new work.

Though several churches give members, there is not a sufficient number to cover the full remuneration of the pastor. So the national board picks up the balance to make the work possible.

There are a number of definite advantages for such a united effort. Usually the new work will receive a church planter who enters his work with excellent references. Before being commissioned to the work, the planter has been interviewed both by the national board and the families in the new church. Even before this there are forms to be filled out. A lengthy resume; autobiography, summary of doctrinal beliefs and a response to the pressing issues of the day must all be submitted. The procedure is similar to an ordination council. A national board must be especially careful of appointees because they are accountable to the annual sessions of the denomination. A thorough screening will provide a good basis for choosing a strong candidate..

The national board requires monthly reports on the progress of the work, including statistics of church attendances, offerings, baptisms and other important items to help the board understand the work and where extra help is needed. This report is followed up with either a letter, a phone call or a personal visit, depending on the situation. Reinforcement of this nature is required for a pastor engaged in church planting. It gives him someone to share ministry burdens with, and he is always assured of a helping hand and a sympathetic heart. He is not alone in the real sense of the word.

Denominational resources are made available to these churches. Such things as Land Acquisition funds, through which property may be purchased ahead of time, can be of great assistance to a new work. When building time arrives, again loans are forthcoming. Experience shows that when a new church puts up a sign to indicate its permanent location, immediately additional families take an interest. The same thing happens when the first unit of a new church has been constructed. People like to participate in a growing organization, and land purchase and erection of buildings generally speak of growth and development.

Denominational boards insist on a certain standard of work.. Reports are generally made of the number of visitation calls, the services planned and carried out and the financial stewardship of the church. Further, prayer requests are made known to supporting churches, generating a great deal of interest and assistance.

The Properties Baptist Church of Calgary, Alberta, got underway in this fashion. Several families from various Fellowship Baptist churches had a series of Bible studies and prayer meetings with Pastor Gerald Meller. It was soon evident that the mixture was good and the group felt the kinship necessary to engage together in starting a new church. This then became a joint project of the Southern Alberta Association, other churches in Alberta and Saskatchewan, and the national Home Mission Board.

There are some drawbacks with this method, of course. The new church loses a little of its autonomy in that the people cannot call a church planter without the endorsement of the candidate by the national board. There is considerable record keeping in order to satisfy those who are putting up the finances. Further, a new church must receive permission before the purchase of property or the erection of a building. These are not negative factors, but rather are intended for the welfare and good of the church.

5. Daughter churches formed through a "Macedonian Call"

There are times when a local church finds itself in real trouble, almost to the point where it must close up and sell its assets to pay off debts. Denominational churches can appeal to their home office, but unaffiliated churches have little recourse but to write to other churches where they might or might not receive a sympathetic ear. Time after time, churches have lost everything and their ministry has been concluded because it was impossible to carry on due to lack of funds, lack of supporting families or mismanagement.

There have been times when such churches have appealed to denominations where they felt kinship and upon receiving a favorable response have had their work maintained. This is really church planting, for without such support the work would have been closed.

Mind you, such support is only forthcoming after careful thought and study of the field. Those responsible for carrying out the inspection insist on having access to all church records, historical accounts, types of ministries in recent years and the relationship existing between remaining members. The physical plant is studied as well as the community and its makeup. Generally the budget is revamped and suggested changes must be carried out in due time.

Riverside Baptist Church, Windsor, Ontario, was an unafflliated church when it ran into a financial crisis in the early 1970s. Their services were down to the sixties in an auditorium that could seat several hundred. Their indebtedness was about $360,000. Pastorless and downhearted, the members turned to Campbell Baptist Church on the other side of Windsor, which in turn involved the national Home Mission Board of The Fellowship of Evangelical Baptist Churches in Canada. An experienced pastor, Alan Silvester, accepted the challenge and Fellowship churches came together to assist. Campbell Baptist responded with a commissioning service of several of its key families. Today, Riverside is a strong, self-supporting church with a high level of missionary commitment.

In December, 1977, eleven members were the only ones left in the former Winnett Memorial Baptist Church, Oakville, Ontario. This was an unaffiliated work. This church was housed in a spacious 350 seat auditorium with an excellent two-story educational wing on a scenic two acre site. However, over a course of time, negative interpersonal relationships prevailed, and gradually people left until eventually the remaining members could no longer maintain a ministry in their lovely building. A Macedonian Call came to the home office of the Fellowship Baptists and to Calvary Baptist Church on the west side of Oakville. Pastor Trevor Baird was most sympathetic and encouraged sixty members to take up the challenge and establish what is today the Chartwell Baptist Church, now a flourishing work.

6. Cooperating versus opposing daughter churches

What kind of a model is this? Well, there are times within an established church when a group of members disagree with the way the church is moving. It may be that the emphasis is too strongly evangelistic, or in some other way does not satisfy this group. Instead of having a split, diplomacy is used, and these members are called upon to start a church more to their own liking, yet cooperating with the parent church. The members of the new work are then satisfied with their own emphasis and are still joined in fellowship with the parent church. A number of case illustrations could be used, but it is best simply to state that such churches do exist.

Examples could also be given of situations where this daughter concept was not encouraged, with the result that the group still left, forming a church strongly opposed to the original ministry.

Several years ago a large church in a community of sixty thousand had reached capacity and prepared to build an even larger auditorium. Several families wanted to start a daughter work with the sponsorship of the main church. A site had been selected and Bible studies were ready to start. The pastor and his associate, however, decided to wait until the new auditorium had been erected. In the meantime an independent pastor came to the city and started a new work, actually purchasing the site that was under consideration by the first church. Today in that city there are two churches, neither having fellowship with the other and competing instead of cooperating.

In another case, a pastor was prepared to start a church in a neighbouring city but felt the time was not right because one of his leading families lived there and if the work got underway he would lose that talented couple. It turned out that another independent pastor came to the city and started a work. The family the pastor had wanted to hold went with the new group, which actually became a church in opposition to his.

All we can conclude is that God is going to build His church today, and we had better not stand in His way.

7. Daughters started through adoption

Many times a church is located in a small community where it just would not be feasible to start a daughter work. This does not need to prevent the church from getting involved. Such churches need to be challenged to look to another province or state where there is a particular need.

Emmanuel Baptist Church, Chatham, Ontario, is a well established congregation without indebtedness. The pastor and people heard about a special need for a new church in Regina, Saskatchewan, some 1500 miles across the country. The Chatham church took the work on and advanced $25,000 to assist with the building fund.

It was a source of real encouragement when Bethel Baptist Church, Kitchener, Ontario, sent a cheque for $10,000 to the newly organized Port of Fellowship Baptist Church, Port Elgin, Ontario.

Pastor Clark Hutchison of Eastside Baptist Church, Marietta, Georgia, sat on the Home Mission Board of the Southern Baptist Convention. At one session there was a report from Pastor Bob Brantley who had started a new church in Victoria, British Columbia. Land costs were high and the church needed $160,000 for the purchase of a suitable site. Clark presented this need to his 3,800 member church in Georgia, and one member asked, "Why don't we take a step of faith and send them the money?"

After several weeks of discussion and prayer, the deacons recommended that their church provide the needed funds to the Canadian church. It is interesting to note that this was done in the midst of their own building program. However, as the pastor said, "Our trust is in Luke 6:38, 'Give and it will be given unto you,' and it has proven true." This has been an inspiration to the giving church as well as to the receivers.

8. Daughters born through relocation

There are situations where a church has worked a community so many times that the law of diminishing returns sets in. Members become restless, wanting to see more happening. Promotion is carried out, homes are visited and great effort is set forth year after year, but all to no avail. Yet there is a guilt complex about moving away and leaving the community without a witness. This problem can be resolved when the major portion of the church relocates, but leaves the facilities to a smaller number of members to maintain the work.

Bethel Chapel in Pointe Claire, Montreal, has for a number of years, been bursting at the seams. This Open Brethren Assembly was running about two hundred people in a very modest building. The nine elders had led the assembly in earnest prayer about the situation and were led of God to consider a relocation on the West Island. They did not want to leave Pointe Claire entirely, however, so one-third of the assembly remained and two-thirds moved out to form the Westview Bible Church. Services got underway on Sunday, September 8, 1985. Within one month the attendances have far exceeded what Bethel Chapel had in its best years.

There are a number of conclusions that can be drawn from the examination of the mother/daughter church concept, in all of its forms. These should be kept in mind whenever a parent church is considering church extension.

Generally speaking, parent/daughter churches will grow numerically. The parent church will have members responding to fill the gaps left, and the ministry will soon refill the vacant pews. At the same time, the new church with its life and vitality will soon generate growth.

Experience also shows that parent/daughter churches will see additional finances come in. From the opening Sunday, the offerings from the combined churches will more than equal what would have been received by the parent church alone. Again this is to be expected because members remaining in the parent church will see the need to give more generously to make up for those who have left to start a new work. At the same time the members of the new church will see so many needs that they will be challenged to meet them with increased financial support.

One needs to remember that a parent church can build and plant at the same time. It does not have to be one or the other. Both can be accomplished successfully and have been many times.

The planting of a daughter church has often been effective in dissolving a negative power block and preventing a church split.

Planting daughter churches tends to develop members and to bring out hidden gifts. It is amazing how many talents of our people lie dormant. Many times of necessity when a group of people leave to start a daughter work, new Sunday school teachers are called for and additional people are needed to serve in official capacities. Hence members who have not been active before will, seeing the urgency of the need, step forward to participate.

Whatever model may be followed, the results of a parenting venture will almost assuredly be positive, both for the mother and the daughter church. Doing God's work in God's way always brings His blessing.

6

Sounds Good, But What Now?

Next to the wedding day, itself, nothing is quite as exciting to a married couple as the birth of a child, especially the first one. As a matter of fact, childbirth is a natural and almost expected occurrence for a married couple. In Ephesians, Paul likens the church to the bride in a marriage relationship with Christ, and if this is so, then reproduction should be an expected event in the life of the church.

Such reproduction becomes even more important when one realizes that with few exceptions, most congregations reach their saturation point within the first decade of their existence. Look over the history of your church. If it is ten years old you will likely begin to trace a slowing in the net gain in membership.

All well and good, you may be saying, but what can an individual member or even the pastor do about it? There are a number of things each individual can do.

You can accept personal evangelistic responsibility for all the people you know. Evangelism begins with you and the people in your own little world, be they family members, relatives, neighbours or associates through work. Dr. Win Arn, President of Church Growth of America, claims that seventy-one percent of church members were introduced to their church by means of a member already within that church. We may conclude, then, that if your neighbour is going to be reached, you are in the best position to reach him.

Pastor Don Robins, while he was serving in Temple Baptist Church in Bedford-Sackville, Nova Scotia, had the joy of baptizing his neighbour. Pastor William Wicks of Fellowship Baptist Church, Mayerthorpe, Alberta, rejoiced when his eleven year-old daughter led a neighbour child to the Lord.

This is where church reproduction begins. One can readily see that if a church had twenty or so members personally witnessing and winning their neighbours to Christ, the attendances would increase to the point where there would be a population explosion. This would of necessity force the church to consider some form of expansion.

All this leads us to consider how a member can be motivated to reach friends, neighbours and relatives. Several years ago the Baptist General Conference introduced "The Circle of Concern." In this ministry concept, members were encouraged to make a list of from one to six families within their sphere of acquaintance, noting as well one major need of their lives. The member would then focus on one of these families and make its members his personal mission. When these needs have been met, the Christian can then include another family. One can readily see that if a person would focus on one or two others, providing friendship and hospitality, praying for them and encouraging them, most likely the opportunity would soon arise to invite them to church and have the invitation accepted. It may appear a slow procedure to narrow your field down to one or two contacts, but actually it is only slow because so few are engaged in an orderly approach to evangelism. There is a tendency to think of reaching your whole community, which is impossible. Unless one narrows down the field to a small number, little will be accomplished.

A church member needs to extend his boundaries beyond his own local church. How? By considering what communities border his church and finding out whether these communities are being adequately served spiritually. This will help him to zero in on the areas surrounding his own local work.

Pastor Robert Holmes of Orangeville Baptist Church, Orangeville, Ontario, looked around the several communities within close proximity and saw East Caledon, some fifteen miles southeast. A survey of the town indicated that projected new growth made the need for an evangelical church imminent.

But he was a pastor, you say. What can a church member do when he becomes conscious of such needs? Share your concern with your pastor and your church. Perhaps the church will be led to open a Bible study and to test the receptiveness of the community. If possible, you could participate in the Bible study cell group. Vacation Bible school could be held during spring break or summer vacation as a means of testing the openness of the community towards your church. Many churches have started a branch work by first using a bus and bringing the people to the parent church until the new work was ready to open. It is true that the bus ministry is not being used today as it was in the 1960s and 70s, but there is still a place for the use of buses, and this is one case where they can assist in opening a new community.

But how can one tell if a community is ripe even if a few do respond to a Bible study or vacation school? First find out how many evangelical churches are in the community. Ascertain Sunday morning attendances. Discover if the churches have outreach ministries by means of regular visitation programs, mailings or other means to reach the people. Study the church buildings to see if they are adequate to serve the area. Try to find out the morale within the congregation. This is an important factor in church growth.

Local schools can be most helpful in providing enrolments, a breakdown of ethnic groups, single parents and population trends. A visit to the municipal planning department will give you information as to potential house starts and future development.

Perhaps an actual example of how such investigation is done would be helpful. Not very long ago the Fellowship Home Mission Board became concerned about a city just north of Toronto. This community of 15,000 was averaging over 200 house starts each year. There were two evangelical churches in town, one averaging eighty in the morning service, the other twenty. Neither church had an effective outreach and both had come to the point of stagnation. One had fine facilities, and the other was housed in an inadequate edifice. In addition, the board discovered that four Fellowship Baptist families were motoring out of the community to attend church. It soon became evident that this was a target area for a new church. Contact was made with the nearest Fellowship church, whose pastor was most sympathetic and took the project to his board and then to the church. One of the deacons has been assigned to the project and Bible studies commenced in the fall of 1985 with a target date of August, 1986, for a church planter to be on site.

Do you dare to ask God for a deep conviction that He wants the lost found and that He wants to use you to find them? Solomon said it well, "Where there is no vision the people perish." People are perishing without Jesus Christ. Yet God in His program of world evangelism has ordained local churches to carry out His mandate. This means that local church members must come to the point of realization that God wants to use them if the lost are to be brought into the fold.

Luke tells us in chapter 19 that when Jesus saw Jerusalem, He wept. Why? Surely one reason was because He saw a religious community dead to the reality of God. Yes, the people of Jerusalem were very religious, marking their holy days, observing the law and carrying out the rituals as prescribed by the priests and scribes. Yet this same city did not recognize its own Messiah.

Our North American culture is a religious one, yet, like Jerusalem, it is dead to the reality of God. North America observes religious days, the Jewish New Year, Christmas, and Easter to name a few. Over fifty percent of the population claims some religious affiliation. Ours is not considered a heathen continent. Yet, when one considers the minimal impact being made by the churches, one wonders if indeed this is not a heathen continent, with secularism as our god.

It must be concluded that North Americans with all their religious trappings are lost without a faith in Jesus Christ. It is time that we pray for the conviction expressed in the familiar chorus of a few years ago:

> Lead me to some soul today,
> And teach me, Lord, just what to say.
> Friends of mine are lost in sin
> And cannot find their way.
> Few there are who seem to care,
> And few there are who pray.
> Melt my heart and fill my life;
> Give me one soul today.

It is important to become knowledgeable in the field of church reproduction. Study principles and procedures by reading various books on the subject. Visit a parent and a daughter church. Ask questions of the leadership. Dig out both the positive and negative sides of the issue. Ask what they would do differently in light of experience. Attend church growth and church planting seminars. A helpful bibliography is given at the end of this chapter, to get you started.

It is amazing the zeal that will be generated as one begins to understand the untold possibilities in the field of church reproduction. The inevitable question seems to be, "Why have we waited so long?" However, better late than never!

You can volunteer to participate in the launching of a new church. It is often a problem to get volunteers to be part of the growing edge of a new church, but if a work is going to be started, participants are required. Why not you? Such decisions must be voluntary. Several churches have made the mistake of drawing a boundary and saying that members who live in the area where the new work is being started should now consider supporting the endeavour. The usual response to such conscription is, "Don't you want me here any more?" It is easy to foster misunderstanding. If you lead the way by coming forward, however, you will encourage others to follow.

Now, let's face the facts. Volunteering for a new work is not easy. You give up all the trappings of a well established church — the robed choir, organ, beautiful pews, Sunday school rooms, spacious auditorium, and all the other things that have been part of your experience. And for what? A cold high school gym. Wooden chairs. An out of tune piano. Restricted space. Yet pioneers are needed if new churches are ever going to get underway. Set the pace. Step out and be counted. Think of the ultimate goal.

Plan now and set your plan in action. Many churches have the desire to start a daughter church, but not just now. The time is not right. Actually, there will never be a time when everything is just right. One pastor, seven years ago, said he wanted to start a daughter work, but not just then because the church was considering a building program and all the families would be needed. Today the church is just the same, with no building in sight, yet it has experienced a great turnover in families in the intervening years.

It is necessary to draw up a schedule and seek by the grace of God to adhere to it. This will help the members to know where the church is going. It will give those families who will eventually form the core of the new church an idea of what offices they may still fill for a time in the mother church. It will also help with financial planning as the mother prepares to help the daughter.

It is wise to ask yourself about your present facilities. If they are not being used to capacity, not even to seventy-five percent, should the church wait until it is stronger? Such a state is not necessarily a deterrent to planning a daughter church. In fact it may serve to awaken dormant members to come forward and shoulder greater responsibility if some of the leaders are commissioned to start a new church.

In one association meeting, several pastors were considering starting a new church in an adjoining town. Two of them expressed the opinion that this should not take place since there was still room in all the churches concerned for more people. "Let's fill our own buildings, first", was their consensus. Fortunately this was not the feeling of the whole group, and the new work did get underway. It is highly unlikely that those people in the other town would ever have come to fill the pews in existing churches when they were determined to meet the needs of their own community. Granted, there are times when it would not be wise for a self-supporting church to launch a new work in their town, particularly if the population is limited and you can get from one side of town to the other in a few minutes. Even in such cases, though, the church might consider an area twenty or thirty miles away where there is a need for an effective witness.

It is important to understand and practise the principle that the local church is the primary agency for church planting. Refrain from doing it on your own, apart from the endorsement of your church. You must remember that your local church is a body of believers, and to function properly a body must be a unified whole with each part working together. It is not wise to go off on your own, apart from the prayerful and moral support of your church.

Why not? For one thing, going it alone can cause division. You have close friends and associates within the body. If the church chooses not to endorse your work you could cause people to take sides and thus divide the congregation.

One business man spoke to the church extension board of his denomination. He was anxious to start a work five miles from the church where he had his membership. Now there was a spiritual vacuum in the community he had chosen. Furthermore, it was a fast developing part of the city with over five hundred house starts in the past and present year in which the work was to start. In the council of the board, the decision was made not to proceed for a number of valid reasons. The man went ahead anyway, and in doing so caused unrest within the church because the board could not endorse his move.

Another problem to consider is that if you go it alone, you may well remain that way for some period of time. Once you have the church's endorsement it is much easier to get people to assist you. Not too many members desire to leave a comfortable pew unless the church is behind the new situation.

There is the financial aspect to consider as well. Without the church's endorsement, you cannot expect full or even partial financial assistance. When the church votes to back an enterprise such as this, however, there is generally a financial commitment that follows. This should not be the primary reason for seeking approval, but it is another benefit.

It may be that the church will not accept your vision to launch out and start a new work. Or the church may react and move much more slowly than you would like. What do you do? You wait. You pray. You seek the peace of God. It may well be that in the providence of God the new work should not start just now. Or on the other hand, it could be that your church is out of touch with church growth. At any rate, you seek the unity of the church before seeking to carry out your own will and vision. Paul talked about spiritual maturity in I Corinthians 3. In the third verse he says that one mark of spiritual maturity is the ability to maintain the unity of the Spirit of God within a local church. Yes, you may wait quite a while before the church votes to move ahead. If you believe that God leads in a local church, however, you can wait for the door to open in due time.

This continues Paul's theme of I Corinthians 3:9 where he declares, "Ye are workers together with God." All too often members have gone their own way, especially in churches which practise local autonomy. Such rugged independence is needed if the project of a new work is to be successful, but it must be exercised within the guidelines of the local church.

This leads us to another principle. When developing a church planting strategy, you must base it on the inexhaustible spiritual resources of God. Too many times faith is not exercised. Some people will not move out unless they can see the end from the beginning — the land, the building, finances for staff and the whole budget of maintaining a church must be forecasted. This is neither practical nor possible. You should not expect to have all your resources for total church reproduction at the outset. New people who will be reached by the new church will carry part of the responsibility. You may not know how the money will come in, or from whom. This is where faith enters the project. You only know that if God is in it, He has the resources and can move people into the community, can draw people to Himself and can lead them to work with you. He is the Lord of the harvest. It is His church, not yours! So if you have the assurance that God is directing, move out in full confidence to start that extension work.

This confidence, though, leaves no room for practising poor stewardship. We must not be reckless with the money God has given us. But there is a point at which the church needs to venture out with expectation, believing God will see it through.

Do not overlook the natural principle of dividing to multiply. Within the human body cells divide to multiply. So it is, too, within the body of the church. The division in such a case is not negative, but rather planned by the church for positive extension ministry. Before long, both segments of the divided body are growing and multiplying.

One prominent business man told us a story about attendance in the church of which he is a member. Seven years ago the auditorium was filled to capacity. Just as it is today. But in the meantime, over the course of those seven years, the church has gained well over one hundred and fifty members and lost the same number because of lack of space. Is that growth? What if seven years ago the church had commissioned even one hundred members to launch a new work? The main church would still be packed out and the new work would, perhaps, have doubled. One ignores the principle of multiplication by division to one's peril.

You can also encourage the development of more bivocational pastors to become involved in church reproduction. Many churches today do not have all the resources needed to carry out reproduction on their own. Yet they see the need. This is where greater use can be made of bivocational church planters. Such men, like the apostle Paul who made tents for a living, are involved in church planting while carrying a secular job to help with financial needs.

Thousands of churches have been organized by tent makers. Judy Touchton commenting on such pastors, said, "From Paul to today, bivocational pastors — the `tentmaking preachers' — have filled church history. They are the worker-priests, the non-stipendary clergy, the `working preachers'."

One such bivocational pastor, now in his fourth church, is Ted Clark. Ted believes God has uniquely called and trained him for the ministry. He is a graduate of Northwest Baptist Theological College and Seminary, Vancouver, B.C. In addition he is a professional chartered accountant. For him this is an ideal combination of skills. In fact, his business has opened doors that otherwise are often closed to pastors.

Does this type of ministry pay off? Well consider for a moment the influence of Ted Clark, starting first in Saskatoon with the Lorne Avenue Baptist Church, followed by a most successful church planting venture at the Hay River Baptist Church in the Northwest Territories. This was succeeded by ministry in Vermilion, Alberta and most recently in Wainwright, Alberta. Through this one man's ministry groups of believers are now ministering in formerly unreached communities.

Denominations need to consider how this concept can be fostered, and how their member churches can minister to these special pastors. At the same time, churches with such pastors must be encouraged to shoulder their part of his support.

Pastors and members need to be on the lookout for men who can fulfill this calling. Just as young men are sought out for the ministry, so we must begin to seek out men in their forties and fifties who have been successful in their line of work and challenge them to take an early retirement in order to enter some line of pastoral or church planting ministry.

In 1978, Pastor James Rendle of Campbell Baptist Church in Windsor, Ontario saw the need of a struggling church several miles from where he was working. He invited one of his leaders, Adrian Crewson, who was at that time treasurer of the Green Giant Corporation of Canada, to assist the church in ministry. This was an opening door for Adrian, and he has continued in such work through the intervening years. Presently he is serving at Eglinton Baptist Church, Toronto, in the same capacity. Without a doubt there are hundreds, if not thousands of gifted men in our churches equipped to reproduce a church.

Yes, as a local church member you have a part to play in the developing of new churches. And when a church is opened from your home church, you can use creativity in the development of prospects. It is important to touch families when they are most receptive. There are experiences in the lives of people that make them more open to the gospel witness than others. The birth of a new baby, a marital crisis, sickness, a job change, death in the family circle, retirement, hospitalization, moving to a new residence, all are events which turn a family's thoughts toward God and His church.

This is the time when members of the local church need to be alert and ready to become that link they need to make actual contact with the church. If we are on the outlook for possibilities, there is no shortage of them. Names of new arrivals can be obtained through the local "Welcome Wagon" hostess. Names of families with new babies are readily available from the local newspaper, and these new arrivals can be enrolled in your church's cradle roll. This gives excellent opportunity for continuing contact with the family. But be sure you have a well-equipped nursery if you are going to reach out to young families.

Enlist the retired people within your membership. These people, now without full daytime responsibilities, are of immeasurable help in letter-writing, follow up, hospitality, and many of the practical aspects of church extension.

Above all, keep in mind that our God is not willing that any should perish. Evangelization through church planting is God's method, and when we embark on such a project we are showing our obedience to Jesus Christ. We are fulfilling the great commission in our day.

Dr. John Alexander White once said, "The world's seven perils could be defined as: politics without principle, wealth without work, pleasure without conscience, knowledge without character, industry without humanity, science without morality and worship without sacrifice." Might we add another, perhaps even greater peril: Christianity without vision. I believe in the eyes of God the lack of vision of His church for extending itself through natural reproduction is perhaps one of the greatest of perils.

Yes, next to the wedding day, nothing is quite as exciting to a married couple as a birth of a child. Why deny your church the excitement of planned parenthood? Start a daughter church today and see God at work!

7

Twenty Questions Answered

1. How can a parent church determine if it can afford to launch a daughter work?

Actually, this question should be turned around. How can a church not afford to start a daughter work? The overall results are so rewarding that such a work should be undertaken as quickly as possible.

However, the initial question remains valid in discussing the affordability of such a project. If the church considers from day one the total cost involved, including such items as pastoral remuneration, land purchase and construction costs of an edifice, such an undertaking would be out of the question.

The church must rather consider the project in steps. Can a Bible study be formed in a certain area? As interest continues, can a pastor of extension be called? With each succeeding step more families become involved, and this brings more financial assistance to cover the increasing costs.

The apostle Paul likens the church to a bride. When entering a marriage relationship, few young couples consider the total costs that will eventually be incurred over years of living together, buying houses, raising a family, etc. And so it should be with the beginning of a new church. You take one step at a time, meeting the financial requirements as they come.

2. Would it not be better to add to the present church building than to start a new work?

Why not do both? Church planting does not need to deter the parent church from growing and developing to the point where larger facilities are needed. The advantage of church planting is that another community is opened up where in all likelihood new people will be reached. Even with an addition to the present building, you will not reach as many in the new community as a new church will.

3. Will starting a daughter church hurt a church financially?

Yes! No question about it. But that's missions. The parent church will be required to give sacrificial support if the new work is going to have sufficient support.

Church planting is as normal as having a family. Over the course of time it takes thousands of dollars to raise a child from birth through college. But parents don't hesitate to make the commitment. Mothering a daughter church is a similar experience, financially. It is costly, but this is true of our total missionary commitment. To send a couple overseas today a church must consider annual support of from $18,000 to $35,000. But overseas missions and church planting both are part of the great commission.

4. How can a good spirit be maintained between the parent and daughter churches?

It is disappointing when negative relationships arise between the two churches. However, parents with growing teenagers sometimes have disagreements, and the same thing is true with mother and daughter churches.

It is important that the two pastors maintain a spirit of transparency between them. They serve as models, and if they can show such a spirit, more than likely the same will prevail between the congregations. Pastors serve as the key to good relationships.

One step to good relations is taken when the parent church provides facilities as needed by the new work. Many churches will share their secretary, office equipment and even supplies to assist the daughter work.

An annual fellowship night with a potluck supper is helpful. Pulpit exchanges show the working together of the leadership. Annual retreats for board members of the two churches can assist in bridging any gaps.

A steady ministry of prayer will perhaps be most effective in preventing an ill spirit from entering into the fellowship. And joint projects in outreach visitation and united evangelistic endeavours, too, foster a spirit of oneness.

5. Will planting a daughter church cause a division within the parent body?

It can, if not handled correctly. For example, if several families desire to start a daughter work and the leadership of the established work seek to block it, there may well be the seeds sown for eventual division.

Yes, in launching a new work there will be families leaving, but this is part of the cost of growth and development. It is somewhat like parents whose growing youth look towards marriage. It must be realized that they will leave home, but they are not lost to the family.

6. How do you assign families to the new church?

You don't! This is a time for motivating families, not conscripting them. You can do this by introducing the need, presenting the challenge and asking families to give it prayerful consideration. Assure them that the new work will have the support of the parent church and that every effort will be made to assist them in the new church.

One way to promote this is to invite families in the area to a series of Bible studies. Another way is to seek out two or three top leaders and have them committed to the project. But nagging, shaming or bribing families will not accomplish your purpose of getting committed people.

7. Should the senior pastor of the parent church become the pastor of the daughter work?

This question rises because of enthusiasm that develops when a new work is under consideration. It is not wise, however, for the senior pastor to leave the parent work in order to pastor the extension ministry. For one thing, he has been called to serve the parent church initially, and when he does resign, he really should leave the area.

A pastor usually has the majority of his people behind him, and if he leaves with the commissioned members, it may well be that too many would choose to relocate with him. This could harm both the parent and the daughter work financially, and seriously undermine the good relationships that would normally prevail.

8. How does a parent church choose an area if there are several locations in need of such a work?

In the first place you need to plan for several daughter churches over a period of time. It may well be that when you launch one, in due time that one may be strong enough to assist with others you may plan in the future.

But how does a church choose one site over others? You must establish certain priorities to be sought in an ideal site, and then work on one site at a time. Research the number of evangelical churches in the area and the strength of those churches. Find out whether one area has more interested families than another; if there is a school or other building that can be rented for church services.

Elmer Towns suggests that a church planter should drive through the neighbourhood and take note of ...

The public schools
The shopping centres
The existing churches
The price and value of homes
The projection of new homes
The size of building lots
Topography
Water, sewage and gas connections
Industrial and other barriers in the neighbourhood
The main arteries and thoroughfares[1]

In addition, get the zoning ordinances of the city to determine restrictions on a proposed church.

9. Is there any type of community that is more responsive than others to a new church?

Yes! A community in transition of a newly developing subdivision is more open to church planting than an established community with an older population. You will often find that in a stable community the school population is declining and people are well set in their ways. If they have a church home, they are unlikely to want to change. If they do not have a church home, it is often difficult to gain their attention.

In a changing community, people are not as set in their ways. They are more open to meeting new people and getting their children involved in a meaningful fellowship.

10. How can a church find out the number of people not churched by evangelical churches?

You can interview all the evangelical pastors of the area or the people who attend these churches, asking for attendance statistics. The local Gideon Camp will furnish you with such statistics from their annual Church Sunday.

The "window survey" method is helpful, too. At the time of morning service, drive around the area checking the number of cars and buses both on the streets and in the parking lots. Since most people do not walk far any more, this figure will give a good estimate of the number of people attending the church.

11. What size population is needed in a given community to start a new work, and how can a church ascertain projected population increases over the next five years?

It is generally agreed that the portion of the population reachable by a conservative church is two percent, including children. If one applies this guideline when choosing a community, a population of under 2,000 would not be able to support a full-time worker without outside assistance (2,000 x .02 is 40 people reachable, 11 to 12 families). On the other hand, a population of 4,000 would be better able to support a full-time pastor and a church development.

Projected increases in population can be calculated from information in the Financial Post. Local municipal offices or Chambers of Commerce can also assist. Even the local school board is a means of obtaining advance information.

12. Is it important to have a Statement of Faith and a constitution early in the life of the daughter church?

Yes. This sets the standard for the people uniting with the membership as the work develops. If it is postponed, several families might come into the work from other churches that are entirely out of fellowship with what the founding families have agreed upon.

The Statement of Faith also serves as a guide for instruction classes. It spells out the distinctives of the new work. The constitution sets up guidelines for workers as well as a standard of conduct to be expected for leadership.

13. What are some ways a new church can become known and reach families in a community?

Newspaper ads will cover a major portion of the community. Visiting municipal offices and meeting the officers will show your interest in their work.

Get acquainted with the various schools and their staff members. Make use of the postman, or leave attractive literature on store counters for free distribution. A visitation blitz can be most helpful or a door to door survey using the contemporary questionnaire approach.

You can also circulate the news of your work through your denominational paper, asking for people to send names of friends and relatives who live in the area.

Some pastors have made use of the telephone, dividing up names of families listed and assigning them to members willing to make calls. It is wise to prepare a printed statement for volunteers to use so there is a standard procedure of introduction and a clear message presented.

Sandwich boards strategically placed, pointing to the location of the services, can be set out on Sundays, at least until the location is familiar.

But the best way to break into a new community is to determine the felt needs of its people. Ruddy Childress, renowned for his ministry of reaching business and professional people in Richmond, Virginia, said, when asked the reason for his breakthrough, "My first concern is with the clients' felt needs, such as trying to save a marriage or overcome a drinking problem." In other words, as we understand the needs of people, we earn the right to meet them and try to help them find the answer to those needs. Of course we recognize that their deepest need is spiritual in nature, but we use a "felt need" to lead us to the meeting of that deepest need. We must meet people where they are if we would lead them to Christ, where we want them to be.

14. Is there any particular time when a new church should be considering erection of a building?

We all recognize that a church is not a building, but is our North American context, a church must in due course have a building. Most of us aspire to home ownership. We tend to collect things. This spills over into the mindset of church members as well. You will soon notice that new churches can get along well for three to five years without their own facilities, but after that families start to look around for a more permanent situation. Very few churches ten years of age exist today without having their own edifice, however large or small.

On the other side of the coin, you can build too fast. Some people have the notion that they need a building to have a great congregation. This is not always true. People need the struggle of working and saving money toward a project to strengthen and unite them. They need a sense of personal participation.

A building programme planned from year three to year six gives the congregation sufficient time to plan the style and design needed for the particular ministry they wish to carry on. Most churches plan their building in stages, often starting with Christian education units and leaving the main auditorium until the second or third phase.

15. How many families are needed to begin a daughter work?

This question can only be given a relative answer, depending on the location, the circumstances and the founding families. Churches have started with only one family or with as many as fifty families or more. More important than the number is the purpose behind the project and the commitment of those who form the founding families. If even a few families have a true vision of the need of a community, let them go and help them in establishing an additional testimony.

16. What about membership?

Members of the parent church leaving for the new work should remain members of the mother church until the new work is organized. People coming into the new church should join the mother congregation if the organization is going to be held up for any length of time. Right from day one, though, it is good to have a select group of spiritual people to serve as an interview committee for members wishing to join the new church.

17. Will it hurt young people to be involved with their families in the move to a daughter church?

It would appear on the surface that taking young people from their friends and placing them in seeming isolation would be a negative factor. This does not have to be so. The young people of the new work can continue to attend the youth meetings of the parent church until they have built up the core of their own organization.

And there are advantages to the young people in a new work. They will have opportunities here to participate in meaningful mission. They will probably experience opportunities to serve that would not be available to them in the parent church because of the large number of potential workers. They will share in the excitement of seeing numerical growth which may not have been the case in the parent church. There will also be stronger motivation to become involved in visitation, evangelism and other forms of outreach as together you seek to develop numerical strength and see people won to Christ.

18. How do you call a pastor for the new work?

One way is to have the church plan the extension work over a span of two to three years, giving them time to call a pastor of extension who will be responsible to encourage families in the launching of the new work with him. This must be handled carefully, but with the approval of the senior pastor it can be highly successful in securing the needed number of interested families.

If you do not have an extension pastor, but several families are ready to start the work, have these families extend a pastoral call with the approval of the parent church.

The pastor of the daughter work needs to be in full harmony with the pastor and congregation of the parent church. This is most important if a foundation is to be laid for future cooperation. This is why the senior pastor and several board members should work with the officers of the new church in the calling of the pastor, if he is not already a staff member of the parent church.

19. Should the new work be a replica of the mother church?

Is a child ever a true replica of its parents? There are characteristics that are somewhat alike, of course, but he or she will have features that are uniquely his own. So it is with a daughter church. It needs to develop its own identity. If it is an exact replica of the parent church, there might well be a question as to the need for its existence in another area. Give the new work liberty, within agreed upon boundaries, to express itself in worship and outreach.

It may be that the parent church has a formal worship service, while the daughter may wish to have less formality. The parent church may still have one united midweek prayer meeting; the daughter may decide upon a series of cottage prayer meetings. Each congregation should be free to take on its own unique personality, to flex its muscles and develop its own strengths.

20. Is it possible for the new church to fail?

Yes, is it altogether possible that the project will fall flat. But it is better to fail trying than not to try at all. Actually, one has no assurance that any new project will always work out. We cannot know the end from the beginning; only God has that capability. Little would ever be accomplished, however, if the fear of failure were allowed to prevail at the outset. Projects such as this must be undertaken with a spirit of faith and expectation, resting on the assurance that our God is able and His purpose is to build His church — through His people.

[1.] Towns, Elmer L., Getting a Church Started, Impact Books, 1975, p. 143.

A Lesson in Church Anatomy

What kind of body can lose an eye and a leg and an ear and maybe a thumb, yet grow them back in a short time?

In what circumstances can that eye, leg, ear and thumb join together and quickly become a new, complete body?

(for answers see end of lesson)

Years ago the Board of Education in London, Ontario paid sone teachers whose job description included teaching on reproduction with the example of the amoeba splitting from the parent body, forming its own unit and eventually, itself, splitting again. I didn't find it particularly inspiring; most young men are not interested in things asexual!

Since those days I haven't taken any more biology courses, but I have found that some of those early principles have a much wider application — even carrying over to church reproduction.

Presently I am the pastor of a daughter church — in fact, it's really a granddaughter! Before I left St. Thomas to come to Kitchener, I was privileged to be on the parent side, and to be involved in founding a now thriving daughter church. On the basis of these experiences, may I give you my personal convictions about church reproduction?

Grandview Baptist Church, Kitchener, Ontario was founded thirteen years ago, largely through the vision of First Baptist Church, Waterloo, and its pastor R. Robinson. About 75 people, including, I am told, most of the music people, many Sunday School teachers, and some of the "best" people left First Baptist. It was an act of faith, since the mother church at that time had an attendance of just over 400. Those who left immediately began to worship in a school in the east end of Kitchener. Three years later they built their own building, and from the beginning they have been known as Grandview Baptist Church, with their own pastor, deacons' board, constitution and goals.

Grandview has been a testimony in the east end of Kitchener those thirteen years, and now is a church where last month the average morning attendance was 350. Because of our own beginnings, we at Grandview are committed to the concept of starting a daughter work when we become large enough to do so. And the fact that our mother church was also a daughter only strengthens that commitment. Fifty years ago, First Baptist, Waterloo, came into being through the vision and sacrifice of Benton Street Baptist Church in Kitchener.

And how did the mother church fare in all this? Despite the loss of personnel sustained by First Baptist, within a month they had "plugged all the holes." People who had not had jobs in the church before became more active, and both groups were blessed. As a matter of fact, attendance at First Baptist is now in the high 600s. Also First Baptist paid almost the entire amount for the four-and-a-half acre lot purchased for Grandview.

The key to this outstanding success lay in the fact that First Baptist sent a large group to found Grandview. From the very beginning they had enough people to be self-sufficient. They didn't have to struggle to get along.

The same thing happened in St. Thomas, Ontario We were crowded at Faith Baptist Church with an attendance of 525-650. On January 1, 1980 about 75 of our people were commissioned to found a new church, Eastwood Baptist, in the eastern part of St. Thomas. Gary Carter, Minister of Education at Faith, became pastor of the new work which immediately began morning and evening services. They were self-supporting and set out to be a witness to the whole of St. Thomas.

In only three years they have grown and worked to the place where they are in their new, attractive building and have completed construction of a 26 unit senior citizens' complex. Faith Baptist, meanwhile, has climbed back up to and exceeded its previous size. Mother and baby are doing well! Once again the parent-daughter concept has worked.

As pastor of Faith, St. Thomas at the time, of course I was nervous at first. I was afraid we would lose our best people — and we did lose some of them. But the interesting thing is the Lord of the Church has filled all the gaps in a very short time. The eyes and the legs, the ears and the thumbs who left have become a complete body. And the body who lost them has now grown new eyes, legs, ears and thumbs.

And so it is as we grow and expand our testimony for Christ. Yes, I've been on both sides of the situation, and I firmly believe there can be few more positive approaches to growth than for a parent church to sponsor a daughter.

Answers:

1) a parent church starting a daughter work

2) a daughter work.

Rev. Donald G. Fitchett Grandview Baptist Church Kitchener, Ontario

www.ingramcontent.com/pod-product-compliance
Lightning Source LLC
Chambersburg PA
CBHW070257100426
42743CB00011B/2252